THIS

CAMPER VAN ROAD TRIP TRAVEL JOURNAL

BELONGS TO

NAME ....

E MAIL ....

MOBILE ....

PLEASE RETURN IF FOUND

CAMPER VAN
ROAD TRIP TRAVEL JOURNAL

DATE .... MILEAGE START ....

START TIME .... MILEAGE END ....

ARRIVAL TIME .... MILEAGE TOTAL ....

CAMPSITE NAME OR ....

WILDCAMPING LOCATION ....

ADDRESS 1 ....

ADDRESS 2 ....

GPS .... POST CODE ....

WHAT3WORDS ....

PHONE ....

E MAIL ....

WEBSITE WWW ....

MY RATING .... OUT OF 10   GOOD VALUE - YES / N0

WEATHER .... TEMPERATURE ....

NUMBER OF NIGHTS HERE .... RECOMMEND - YES / NO

DAILY COSTS		TODAY'S HIGHLIGHTS
SITE FEES	£ .	....
FUEL	£ .	....
LPG GAS	£ .	....
GROCERIES	£ .	....
EATING OUT	£ .	....
ENTERTAINMENT	£ .	....
OTHER COSTS	£ .	....
....	£ .	....
....	£ .	....

TOMORROW'S PLAN

....

....

....

....

....

CAMPER VAN
ROAD TRIP TRAVEL JOURNAL

DATE .... MILEAGE START ....

START TIME .... MILEAGE END ....

ARRIVAL TIME .... MILEAGE TOTAL ....

CAMPSITE NAME OR ....

WILDCAMPING LOCATION ....

ADDRESS 1 ....

ADDRESS 2 ....

GPS .... POST CODE ....

WHAT3WORDS ....

PHONE ....

E MAIL ....

WEBSITE WWW ....

MY RATING .... OUT OF 10   GOOD VALUE - YES / N0

WEATHER .... TEMPERATURE ....

NUMBER OF NIGHTS HERE .... RECOMMEND - YES / NO

DAILY COSTS		TODAY'S HIGHLIGHTS
SITE FEES	£ .	....
FUEL	£ .	....
LPG GAS	£ .	....
GROCERIES	£ .	....
EATING OUT	£ .	....
ENTERTAINMENT	£ .	....
OTHER COSTS	£ .	....
....	£ .	....
....	£ .	....

TOMORROW'S PLAN

....

....

....

....

....

CAMPER VAN
ROAD TRIP TRAVEL JOURNAL

DATE .... MILEAGE START ....

START TIME .... MILEAGE END ....

ARRIVAL TIME .... MILEAGE TOTAL ....

CAMPSITE NAME OR ....

WILDCAMPING LOCATION ....

ADDRESS 1 ....

ADDRESS 2 ....

GPS .... POST CODE ....

WHAT3WORDS ....

PHONE ....

E MAIL ....

WEBSITE WWW ....

MY RATING .... OUT OF 10   GOOD VALUE - YES / N0

WEATHER .... TEMPERATURE ....

NUMBER OF NIGHTS HERE .... RECOMMEND - YES / NO

DAILY COSTS		TODAY'S HIGHLIGHTS
SITE FEES	£ .	....
FUEL	£ .	....
LPG GAS	£ .	....
GROCERIES	£ .	....
EATING OUT	£ .	....
ENTERTAINMENT	£ .	....
OTHER COSTS	£ .	....
....	£ .	....
....	£ .	

TOMORROW'S PLAN

....

....

....

....

....

CAMPER VAN
ROAD TRIP TRAVEL JOURNAL

DATE .... MILEAGE START ....

START TIME .... MILEAGE END ....

ARRIVAL TIME .... MILEAGE TOTAL ....

CAMPSITE NAME OR ....

WILDCAMPING LOCATION ....

ADDRESS 1 ....

ADDRESS 2 ....

GPS .... POST CODE ....

WHAT3WORDS ....

PHONE ....

E MAIL ....

WEBSITE WWW ....

MY RATING .... OUT OF 10   GOOD VALUE - YES / N0

WEATHER .... TEMPERATURE ....

NUMBER OF NIGHTS HERE .... RECOMMEND - YES / NO

DAILY COSTS		TODAY'S HIGHLIGHTS
SITE FEES	£ .	....
FUEL	£ .	....
LPG GAS	£ .	....
GROCERIES	£ .	....
EATING OUT	£ .	....
ENTERTAINMENT	£ .	....
OTHER COSTS	£ .	....
....	£ .	....
....	£ .	....

TOMORROW'S PLAN

....

....

....

....

....

CAMPER VAN
ROAD TRIP TRAVEL JOURNAL

DATE .... MILEAGE START ....

START TIME .... MILEAGE END ....

ARRIVAL TIME .... MILEAGE TOTAL ....

CAMPSITE NAME OR ....

WILDCAMPING LOCATION ....

ADDRESS 1 ....

ADDRESS 2 ....

GPS .... POST CODE ....

WHAT3WORDS ....

PHONE ....

E MAIL ....

WEBSITE WWW ....

MY RATING .... OUT OF 10   GOOD VALUE - YES / N0

WEATHER .... TEMPERATURE ....

NUMBER OF NIGHTS HERE .... RECOMMEND - YES / NO

DAILY COSTS	TODAY'S HIGHLIGHTS
SITE FEES £ .	....
FUEL £ .	....
LPG GAS £ .	....
GROCERIES £ .	....
EATING OUT £ .	....
ENTERTAINMENT £ .	....
OTHER COSTS £ .	....
.... £ .	....
.... £ .	

TOMORROW'S PLAN

....

....

....

....

....

CAMPER VAN
ROAD TRIP TRAVEL JOURNAL

DATE .... MILEAGE START ....

START TIME .... MILEAGE END ....

ARRIVAL TIME .... MILEAGE TOTAL ....

CAMPSITE NAME OR ....

WILDCAMPING LOCATION ....

ADDRESS 1 ....

ADDRESS 2 ....

GPS .... POST CODE ....

WHAT3WORDS ....

PHONE ....

E MAIL ....

WEBSITE WWW ....

MY RATING .... OUT OF 10   GOOD VALUE - YES / N0

WEATHER .... TEMPERATURE ....

NUMBER OF NIGHTS HERE .... RECOMMEND - YES / NO

DAILY COSTS	TODAY'S HIGHLIGHTS
SITE FEES £ .	....
FUEL £ .	....
LPG GAS £ .	....
GROCERIES £ .	....
EATING OUT £ .	....
ENTERTAINMENT £ .	....
OTHER COSTS £ .	....
.... £ .	....
.... £ .	....

TOMORROW'S PLAN

....

....

....

....

....

CAMPER VAN
ROAD TRIP TRAVEL JOURNAL

DATE .... MILEAGE START ....

START TIME .... MILEAGE END ....

ARRIVAL TIME .... MILEAGE TOTAL ....

CAMPSITE NAME OR ....

WILDCAMPING LOCATION ....

ADDRESS 1 ....

ADDRESS 2 ....

GPS .... POST CODE ....

WHAT3WORDS ....

PHONE ....

E MAIL ....

WEBSITE WWW ....

MY RATING .... OUT OF 10   GOOD VALUE - YES / N0

WEATHER .... TEMPERATURE ....

NUMBER OF NIGHTS HERE .... RECOMMEND - YES / NO

DAILY COSTS		TODAY'S HIGHLIGHTS
SITE FEES	£ .	....
FUEL	£ .	....
LPG GAS	£ .	....
GROCERIES	£ .	....
EATING OUT	£ .	....
ENTERTAINMENT	£ .	....
OTHER COSTS	£ .	....
....	£ .	....
....	£ .	

TOMORROW'S PLAN

....

....

....

....

....

CAMPER VAN
ROAD TRIP TRAVEL JOURNAL

DATE .... MILEAGE START ....

START TIME .... MILEAGE END ....

ARRIVAL TIME .... MILEAGE TOTAL ....

CAMPSITE NAME OR ....

WILDCAMPING LOCATION ....

ADDRESS 1 ....

ADDRESS 2 ....

GPS .... POST CODE ....

WHAT3WORDS ....

PHONE ....

E MAIL ....

WEBSITE WWW ....

MY RATING .... OUT OF 10   GOOD VALUE - YES / N0

WEATHER .... TEMPERATURE ....

NUMBER OF NIGHTS HERE .... RECOMMEND - YES / NO

DAILY COSTS		TODAY'S HIGHLIGHTS
SITE FEES	£ .	....
FUEL	£ .	....
LPG GAS	£ .	....
GROCERIES	£ .	....
EATING OUT	£ .	....
ENTERTAINMENT	£ .	....
OTHER COSTS	£ .	....
....	£ .	....
....	£ .	....

TOMORROW'S PLAN

....

....

....

....

....

CAMPER VAN
ROAD TRIP TRAVEL JOURNAL

DATE ....   MILEAGE START ····················

START TIME ....   MILEAGE END ....

ARRIVAL TIME ....   MILEAGE TOTAL ....

CAMPSITE NAME OR ....

WILDCAMPING LOCATION ....

ADDRESS 1 ....

ADDRESS 2 ....

GPS .... POST CODE ....

WHAT3WORDS ....

PHONE ....

E MAIL ....

WEBSITE WWW ....

MY RATING .... OUT OF 10   GOOD VALUE - YES / N0

WEATHER .... TEMPERATURE ....

NUMBER OF NIGHTS HERE .... RECOMMEND - YES / NO

DAILY COSTS		TODAY'S HIGHLIGHTS
SITE FEES	£ .	....
FUEL	£ .	....
LPG GAS	£ .	....
GROCERIES	£ .	....
EATING OUT	£ .	....
ENTERTAINMENT	£ .	....
OTHER COSTS	£ .	....
....	£ .	....
....	£ .	....

TOMORROW'S PLAN

....

....

....

....

....

CAMPER VAN
ROAD TRIP TRAVEL JOURNAL

DATE .... MILEAGE START ....

START TIME .... MILEAGE END ....

ARRIVAL TIME .... MILEAGE TOTAL ....

CAMPSITE NAME OR ....

WILDCAMPING LOCATION ....

ADDRESS 1 ....

ADDRESS 2 ....

GPS .... POST CODE ....

WHAT3WORDS ....

PHONE ....

E MAIL ....

WEBSITE WWW ....

MY RATING .... OUT OF 10   GOOD VALUE - YES / N0

WEATHER .... TEMPERATURE ....

NUMBER OF NIGHTS HERE .... RECOMMEND - YES / NO

DAILY COSTS	TODAY'S HIGHLIGHTS
SITE FEES £ .	....
FUEL £ .	....
LPG GAS £ .	....
GROCERIES £ .	....
EATING OUT £ .	....
ENTERTAINMENT £ .	....
OTHER COSTS £ .	....
.... £ .	....
.... £ .	....

TOMORROW'S PLAN

....

....

....

....

....

CAMPER VAN
ROAD TRIP TRAVEL JOURNAL

DATE .... MILEAGE START ....

START TIME .... MILEAGE END ....

ARRIVAL TIME .... MILEAGE TOTAL ....

CAMPSITE NAME OR ....

WILDCAMPING LOCATION ....

ADDRESS 1 ....

ADDRESS 2 ....

GPS .... POST CODE ....

WHAT3WORDS ....

PHONE ....

E MAIL ....

WEBSITE WWW ....

MY RATING .... OUT OF 10   GOOD VALUE - YES / N0

WEATHER .... TEMPERATURE ....

NUMBER OF NIGHTS HERE .... RECOMMEND - YES / NO

DAILY COSTS

SITE FEES £ .

FUEL £ .

LPG GAS £ .

GROCERIES £ .

EATING OUT £ .

ENTERTAINMENT £ .

OTHER COSTS £ .

.... £ .

.... £ .

TODAY'S HIGHLIGHTS

....

....

....

....

....

....

....

TOMORROW'S PLAN

....

....

....

....

....

CAMPER VAN
ROAD TRIP TRAVEL JOURNAL

DATE ....   MILEAGE START ....

START TIME ....   MILEAGE END ....

ARRIVAL TIME ....   MILEAGE TOTAL ....

CAMPSITE NAME OR ....

WILDCAMPING LOCATION ....

ADDRESS 1 ....

ADDRESS 2 ....

GPS .... POST CODE ....

WHAT3WORDS ....

PHONE ....

E MAIL ....

WEBSITE WWW ....

MY RATING .... OUT OF 10   GOOD VALUE - YES / N0

WEATHER .... TEMPERATURE ....

NUMBER OF NIGHTS HERE .... RECOMMEND - YES / NO

DAILY COSTS	TODAY'S HIGHLIGHTS
SITE FEES £ .	....
FUEL £ .	....
LPG GAS £ .	....
GROCERIES £ .	....
EATING OUT £ .	....
ENTERTAINMENT £ .	....
OTHER COSTS £ .	....
.... £ .	....
.... £ .	....

TOMORROW'S PLAN

....

....

....

....

....

CAMPER VAN
ROAD TRIP TRAVEL JOURNAL

DATE ....   MILEAGE START ....

START TIME ....   MILEAGE END ....

ARRIVAL TIME ....   MILEAGE TOTAL ....

CAMPSITE NAME OR ....

WILDCAMPING LOCATION ....

ADDRESS 1 ....

ADDRESS 2 ....

GPS .... POST CODE ....

WHAT3WORDS ....

PHONE ....

E MAIL ....

WEBSITE WWW ....

MY RATING .... OUT OF 10   GOOD VALUE - YES / N0

WEATHER .... TEMPERATURE ....

NUMBER OF NIGHTS HERE .... RECOMMEND - YES / NO

DAILY COSTS		TODAY'S HIGHLIGHTS
SITE FEES	£ .	....
FUEL	£ .	....
LPG GAS	£ .	....
GROCERIES	£ .	....
EATING OUT	£ .	....
ENTERTAINMENT	£ .	....
OTHER COSTS	£ .	....
....	£ .	....
....	£ .	....

TOMORROW'S PLAN

....

....

....

....

....

CAMPER VAN
ROAD TRIP TRAVEL JOURNAL

DATE .... MILEAGE START ....

START TIME .... MILEAGE END ....

ARRIVAL TIME .... MILEAGE TOTAL ....

CAMPSITE NAME OR ....
WILDCAMPING LOCATION ....
ADDRESS 1 ....
ADDRESS 2 ....
GPS .... POST CODE ....
WHAT3WORDS ....
PHONE ....
E MAIL ....
WEBSITE WWW ....
MY RATING .... OUT OF 10   GOOD VALUE - YES / N0
WEATHER .... TEMPERATURE ....
NUMBER OF NIGHTS HERE .... RECOMMEND - YES / NO

DAILY COSTS

SITE FEES	£ .
FUEL	£ .
LPG GAS	£ .
GROCERIES	£ .
EATING OUT	£ .
ENTERTAINMENT	£ .
OTHER COSTS	£ .
....	£ .
....	£ .

TODAY'S HIGHLIGHTS

....
....
....
....
....
....
....
....

TOMORROW'S PLAN

....
....
....
....
....

CAMPER VAN
ROAD TRIP TRAVEL JOURNAL

DATE .... MILEAGE START ....

START TIME .... MILEAGE END ....

ARRIVAL TIME .... MILEAGE TOTAL ....

CAMPSITE NAME OR ....

WILDCAMPING LOCATION ....

ADDRESS 1 ....

ADDRESS 2 ....

GPS .... POST CODE ....

WHAT3WORDS ....

PHONE ....

E MAIL ....

WEBSITE WWW ....

MY RATING .... OUT OF 10   GOOD VALUE - YES / N0

WEATHER .... TEMPERATURE ....

NUMBER OF NIGHTS HERE .... RECOMMEND - YES / NO

DAILY COSTS		TODAY'S HIGHLIGHTS
SITE FEES	£ .	....
FUEL	£ .	....
LPG GAS	£ .	....
GROCERIES	£ .	....
EATING OUT	£ .	....
ENTERTAINMENT	£ .	....
OTHER COSTS	£ .	....
....	£ .	....
....	£ .	....

TOMORROW'S PLAN

....

....

....

....

....

CAMPER VAN
ROAD TRIP TRAVEL JOURNAL

DATE .... MILEAGE START ....

START TIME .... MILEAGE END ....

ARRIVAL TIME .... MILEAGE TOTAL ....

CAMPSITE NAME OR ....

WILDCAMPING LOCATION ....

ADDRESS 1 ....

ADDRESS 2 ....

GPS .... POST CODE ....

WHAT3WORDS ....

PHONE ....

E MAIL ....

WEBSITE WWW ....

MY RATING .... OUT OF 10   GOOD VALUE - YES / N0

WEATHER .... TEMPERATURE ....

NUMBER OF NIGHTS HERE .... RECOMMEND - YES / NO

DAILY COSTS		TODAY'S HIGHLIGHTS
SITE FEES	£ .	....
FUEL	£ .	....
LPG GAS	£ .	....
GROCERIES	£ .	....
EATING OUT	£ .	....
ENTERTAINMENT	£ .	....
OTHER COSTS	£ .	....
....	£ .	....
....	£ .	....

TOMORROW'S PLAN

....

....

....

....

....

CAMPER VAN
ROAD TRIP TRAVEL JOURNAL

DATE .... MILEAGE START ....

START TIME .... MILEAGE END ....

ARRIVAL TIME .... MILEAGE TOTAL ....

CAMPSITE NAME OR ....

WILDCAMPING LOCATION ....

ADDRESS 1 ....

ADDRESS 2 ....

GPS .... POST CODE ....

WHAT3WORDS ....

PHONE ....

E MAIL ....

WEBSITE WWW ....

MY RATING .... OUT OF 10   GOOD VALUE - YES / NO

WEATHER .... TEMPERATURE ....

NUMBER OF NIGHTS HERE .... RECOMMEND - YES / NO

DAILY COSTS

SITE FEES   £   .

FUEL   £   .

LPG GAS   £   .

GROCERIES   £   .

EATING OUT   £   .

ENTERTAINMENT   £   .

OTHER COSTS   £   .

.... £   .

.... £   .

TODAY'S HIGHLIGHTS

....

....

....

....

....

....

....

....

TOMORROW'S PLAN

....

....

....

....

....

CAMPER VAN
ROAD TRIP TRAVEL JOURNAL

DATE .... MILEAGE START ....

START TIME .... MILEAGE END ....

ARRIVAL TIME .... MILEAGE TOTAL ....

CAMPSITE NAME OR ....

WILDCAMPING LOCATION ....

ADDRESS 1 ....

ADDRESS 2 ....

GPS .... POST CODE ....

WHAT3WORDS ....

PHONE ....

E MAIL ....

WEBSITE WWW ....

MY RATING .... OUT OF 10   GOOD VALUE - YES / N0

WEATHER .... TEMPERATURE ....

NUMBER OF NIGHTS HERE .... RECOMMEND - YES / NO

DAILY COSTS

SITE FEES   £ .

FUEL   £ .

LPG GAS   £ .

GROCERIES   £ .

EATING OUT   £ .

ENTERTAINMENT   £ .

OTHER COSTS   £ .

.... £ .

.... £ .

TODAY'S HIGHLIGHTS

....

....

....

....

....

....

....

....

TOMORROW'S PLAN

....

....

....

....

....

CAMPER VAN
ROAD TRIP TRAVEL JOURNAL

DATE .... MILEAGE START ....

START TIME .... MILEAGE END ....

ARRIVAL TIME .... MILEAGE TOTAL ....

CAMPSITE NAME OR ....

WILDCAMPING LOCATION ....

ADDRESS 1 ....

ADDRESS 2 ....

GPS .... POST CODE ....

WHAT3WORDS ....

PHONE ....

E MAIL ....

WEBSITE WWW ....

MY RATING .... OUT OF 10   GOOD VALUE - YES / N0

WEATHER .... TEMPERATURE ....

NUMBER OF NIGHTS HERE .... RECOMMEND - YES / NO

DAILY COSTS	TODAY'S HIGHLIGHTS
SITE FEES £ .	....
FUEL £ .	....
LPG GAS £ .	....
GROCERIES £ .	....
EATING OUT £ .	....
ENTERTAINMENT £ .	....
OTHER COSTS £ .	....
.... £ .	....
.... £ .	....

TOMORROW'S PLAN

....

....

....

....

....

CAMPER VAN
ROAD TRIP TRAVEL JOURNAL

DATE .... MILEAGE START ....

START TIME .... MILEAGE END ....

ARRIVAL TIME .... MILEAGE TOTAL ....

CAMPSITE NAME OR ....

WILDCAMPING LOCATION ....

ADDRESS 1 ....

ADDRESS 2 ....

GPS .... POST CODE ....

WHAT3WORDS ....

PHONE ....

E MAIL ....

WEBSITE WWW ....

MY RATING .... OUT OF 10   GOOD VALUE - YES / NO

WEATHER .... TEMPERATURE ....

NUMBER OF NIGHTS HERE .... RECOMMEND - YES / NO

DAILY COSTS

SITE FEES   £   .

FUEL   £   .

LPG GAS   £   .

GROCERIES   £   .

EATING OUT   £   .

ENTERTAINMENT £ .

OTHER COSTS £   .

.... £   .

.... £   .

TODAY'S HIGHLIGHTS

....

....

....

....

....

....

....

....

TOMORROW'S PLAN

....

....

....

....

....

CAMPER VAN
ROAD TRIP TRAVEL JOURNAL

DATE .... MILEAGE START ....

START TIME .... MILEAGE END ....

ARRIVAL TIME .... MILEAGE TOTAL ....

CAMPSITE NAME OR ....

WILDCAMPING LOCATION ....

ADDRESS 1 ....

ADDRESS 2 ....

GPS .... POST CODE ....

WHAT3WORDS ....

PHONE ....

E MAIL ....

WEBSITE WWW ....

MY RATING .... OUT OF 10   GOOD VALUE - YES / N0

WEATHER .... TEMPERATURE ....

NUMBER OF NIGHTS HERE .... RECOMMEND - YES / NO

DAILY COSTS		TODAY'S HIGHLIGHTS
SITE FEES	£ .	....
FUEL	£ .	....
LPG GAS	£ .	....
GROCERIES	£ .	....
EATING OUT	£ .	....
ENTERTAINMENT	£ .	....
OTHER COSTS	£ .	....
....	£ .	....
....	£ .	....

TOMORROW'S PLAN

....

....

....

....

....

CAMPER VAN
ROAD TRIP TRAVEL JOURNAL

DATE .... MILEAGE START ....

START TIME .... MILEAGE END ....

ARRIVAL TIME .... MILEAGE TOTAL ....

CAMPSITE NAME OR ....

WILDCAMPING LOCATION ....

ADDRESS 1 ....

ADDRESS 2 ....

GPS .... POST CODE ....

WHAT3WORDS ....

PHONE ....

E MAIL ....

WEBSITE WWW ....

MY RATING .... OUT OF 10   GOOD VALUE - YES / N0

WEATHER .... TEMPERATURE ....

NUMBER OF NIGHTS HERE .... RECOMMEND - YES / NO

DAILY COSTS		TODAY'S HIGHLIGHTS
SITE FEES	£ .	....
FUEL	£ .	....
LPG GAS	£ .	....
GROCERIES	£ .	....
EATING OUT	£ .	....
ENTERTAINMENT	£ .	....
OTHER COSTS	£ .	....
....	£ .	....
....	£ .	....

TOMORROW'S PLAN

....

....

....

....

....

CAMPER VAN
ROAD TRIP TRAVEL JOURNAL

DATE .... MILEAGE START ....

START TIME .... MILEAGE END ....

ARRIVAL TIME .... MILEAGE TOTAL ....

CAMPSITE NAME OR ....

WILDCAMPING LOCATION ....

ADDRESS 1 ....

ADDRESS 2 ....

GPS .... POST CODE ....

WHAT3WORDS ....

PHONE ....

E MAIL ....

WEBSITE WWW ....

MY RATING .... OUT OF 10   GOOD VALUE - YES / N0

WEATHER .... TEMPERATURE ....

NUMBER OF NIGHTS HERE .... RECOMMEND - YES / NO

DAILY COSTS	TODAY'S HIGHLIGHTS
SITE FEES £ .	....
FUEL £ .	....
LPG GAS £ .	....
GROCERIES £ .	....
EATING OUT £ .	....
ENTERTAINMENT £ .	....
OTHER COSTS £ .	....
.... £ .	....
.... £ .	

TOMORROW'S PLAN

....

....

....

....

....

CAMPER VAN
ROAD TRIP TRAVEL JOURNAL

DATE .... MILEAGE START ....

START TIME .... MILEAGE END ....

ARRIVAL TIME .... MILEAGE TOTAL ....

CAMPSITE NAME OR ....

WILDCAMPING LOCATION ....

ADDRESS 1 ....

ADDRESS 2 ....

GPS .... POST CODE ....

WHAT3WORDS ....

PHONE ....

E MAIL ....

WEBSITE WWW ....

MY RATING .... OUT OF 10   GOOD VALUE - YES / N0

WEATHER .... TEMPERATURE ....

NUMBER OF NIGHTS HERE .... RECOMMEND - YES / NO

DAILY COSTS	TODAY'S HIGHLIGHTS
SITE FEES £ .	....
FUEL £ .	....
LPG GAS £ .	....
GROCERIES £ .	....
EATING OUT £ .	....
ENTERTAINMENT £ .	....
OTHER COSTS £ .	....
.... £ .	....
.... £ .	....

TOMORROW'S PLAN

....

....

....

....

....

CAMPER VAN
ROAD TRIP TRAVEL JOURNAL

DATE ....   MILEAGE START ....

START TIME ....   MILEAGE END ....

ARRIVAL TIME ....   MILEAGE TOTAL ....

CAMPSITE NAME OR ....

WILDCAMPING LOCATION ....

ADDRESS 1 ....

ADDRESS 2 ....

GPS .... POST CODE ....

WHAT3WORDS ....

PHONE ....

E MAIL ....

WEBSITE WWW ....

MY RATING .... OUT OF 10   GOOD VALUE - YES / N0

WEATHER .... TEMPERATURE ....

NUMBER OF NIGHTS HERE .... RECOMMEND - YES / NO

DAILY COSTS		TODAY'S HIGHLIGHTS
SITE FEES	£ .	....
FUEL	£ .	....
LPG GAS	£ .	....
GROCERIES	£ .	....
EATING OUT	£ .	....
ENTERTAINMENT	£ .	....
OTHER COSTS	£ .	....
....	£ .	....
....	£ .	....

TOMORROW'S PLAN

....

....

....

....

....

CAMPER VAN
ROAD TRIP TRAVEL JOURNAL

DATE .... MILEAGE START ....

START TIME .... MILEAGE END ....

ARRIVAL TIME .... MILEAGE TOTAL ....

CAMPSITE NAME OR ....

WILDCAMPING LOCATION ....

ADDRESS 1 ....

ADDRESS 2 ....

GPS .... POST CODE ....

WHAT3WORDS ....

PHONE ....

E MAIL ....

WEBSITE WWW ....

MY RATING .... OUT OF 10   GOOD VALUE - YES / N0

WEATHER .... TEMPERATURE ....

NUMBER OF NIGHTS HERE .... RECOMMEND - YES / NO

DAILY COSTS		TODAY'S HIGHLIGHTS
SITE FEES	£ .	....
FUEL	£ .	....
LPG GAS	£ .	....
GROCERIES	£ .	....
EATING OUT	£ .	....
ENTERTAINMENT	£ .	....
OTHER COSTS	£ .	....
....	£ .	....
....	£ .	....

TOMORROW'S PLAN

....

....

....

....

....

CAMPER VAN
ROAD TRIP TRAVEL JOURNAL

DATE ....   MILEAGE START ....

START TIME ....   MILEAGE END ....

ARRIVAL TIME ....   MILEAGE TOTAL ....

CAMPSITE NAME OR ....

WILDCAMPING LOCATION ....

ADDRESS 1 ....

ADDRESS 2 ....

GPS .... POST CODE ....

WHAT3WORDS ....

PHONE ....

E MAIL ....

WEBSITE WWW ....

MY RATING .... OUT OF 10   GOOD VALUE - YES / N0

WEATHER .... TEMPERATURE ....

NUMBER OF NIGHTS HERE .... RECOMMEND - YES / NO

DAILY COSTS	TODAY'S HIGHLIGHTS
SITE FEES £ .	....
FUEL £ .	....
LPG GAS £ .	....
GROCERIES £ .	....
EATING OUT £ .	....
ENTERTAINMENT £ .	....
OTHER COSTS £ .	....
.... £ .	....
.... £ .	....

TOMORROW'S PLAN

....

....

....

....

....

CAMPER VAN
ROAD TRIP TRAVEL JOURNAL

DATE .... MILEAGE START ....

START TIME .... MILEAGE END ....

ARRIVAL TIME .... MILEAGE TOTAL ....

CAMPSITE NAME OR ....

WILDCAMPING LOCATION ....

ADDRESS 1 ....

ADDRESS 2 ....

GPS .... POST CODE ....

WHAT3WORDS ....

PHONE ....

E MAIL ....

WEBSITE WWW ....

MY RATING .... OUT OF 10   GOOD VALUE - YES / N0

WEATHER .... TEMPERATURE ....

NUMBER OF NIGHTS HERE .... RECOMMEND - YES / NO

DAILY COSTS		TODAY'S HIGHLIGHTS
SITE FEES	£ .	....
FUEL	£ .	....
LPG GAS	£ .	....
GROCERIES	£ .	....
EATING OUT	£ .	....
ENTERTAINMENT	£ .	....
OTHER COSTS	£ .	....
....	£ .	....
....	£ .	....

TOMORROW'S PLAN

....

....

....

....

....

CAMPER VAN
ROAD TRIP TRAVEL JOURNAL

DATE .... MILEAGE START ....

START TIME .... MILEAGE END ....

ARRIVAL TIME .... MILEAGE TOTAL ....

CAMPSITE NAME OR ....

WILDCAMPING LOCATION ....

ADDRESS 1 ....

ADDRESS 2 ....

GPS .... POST CODE ....

WHAT3WORDS ....

PHONE ....

E MAIL ....

WEBSITE WWW ....

MY RATING .... OUT OF 10   GOOD VALUE - YES / N0

WEATHER .... TEMPERATURE ....

NUMBER OF NIGHTS HERE .... RECOMMEND - YES / NO

DAILY COSTS

SITE FEES   £   .

FUEL   £   .

LPG GAS   £   .

GROCERIES   £   .

EATING OUT   £   .

ENTERTAINMENT   £   .

OTHER COSTS   £   .

....   £   .

....   £   .

TODAY'S HIGHLIGHTS

....

....

....

....

....

....

....

....

TOMORROW'S PLAN

....

....

....

....

....

CAMPER VAN
ROAD TRIP TRAVEL JOURNAL

DATE .... MILEAGE START ....

START TIME .... MILEAGE END ....

ARRIVAL TIME .... MILEAGE TOTAL ....

CAMPSITE NAME OR ....

WILDCAMPING LOCATION ....

ADDRESS 1 ....

ADDRESS 2 ....

GPS .... POST CODE ....

WHAT3WORDS ....

PHONE ....

E MAIL ....

WEBSITE WWW ....

MY RATING .... OUT OF 10   GOOD VALUE - YES / N0

WEATHER .... TEMPERATURE ....

NUMBER OF NIGHTS HERE .... RECOMMEND - YES / NO

DAILY COSTS		TODAY'S HIGHLIGHTS
SITE FEES	£ .	....
FUEL	£ .	....
LPG GAS	£ .	....
GROCERIES	£ .	....
EATING OUT	£ .	....
ENTERTAINMENT	£ .	....
OTHER COSTS	£ .	....
....	£ .	....
....	£ .	....

TOMORROW'S PLAN

....

....

....

....

....

CAMPER VAN
ROAD TRIP TRAVEL JOURNAL

DATE .... MILEAGE START ....

START TIME .... MILEAGE END ....

ARRIVAL TIME .... MILEAGE TOTAL ....

CAMPSITE NAME OR ....

WILDCAMPING LOCATION ....

ADDRESS 1 ....

ADDRESS 2 ....

GPS .... POST CODE ....

WHAT3WORDS ....

PHONE ....

E MAIL ....

WEBSITE WWW ....

MY RATING .... OUT OF 10   GOOD VALUE - YES / NO

WEATHER .... TEMPERATURE ....

NUMBER OF NIGHTS HERE .... RECOMMEND - YES / NO

DAILY COSTS		TODAY'S HIGHLIGHTS
SITE FEES	£ .	....
FUEL	£ .	....
LPG GAS	£ .	....
GROCERIES	£ .	....
EATING OUT	£ .	....
ENTERTAINMENT	£ .	....
OTHER COSTS	£ .	....
....	£ .	....
....	£ .	....

TOMORROW'S PLAN

....

....

....

....

....

CAMPER VAN
ROAD TRIP TRAVEL JOURNAL

DATE .... MILEAGE START ....

START TIME .... MILEAGE END ....

ARRIVAL TIME .... MILEAGE TOTAL ....

CAMPSITE NAME OR ....

WILDCAMPING LOCATION ....

ADDRESS 1 ....

ADDRESS 2 ....

GPS .... POST CODE ....

WHAT3WORDS ....

PHONE ....

E MAIL ....

WEBSITE WWW ....

MY RATING .... OUT OF 10   GOOD VALUE - YES / N0

WEATHER .... TEMPERATURE ....

NUMBER OF NIGHTS HERE .... RECOMMEND - YES / NO

DAILY COSTS		TODAY'S HIGHLIGHTS
SITE FEES	£ .	....
FUEL	£ .	....
LPG GAS	£ .	....
GROCERIES	£ .	....
EATING OUT	£ .	....
ENTERTAINMENT	£ .	....
OTHER COSTS	£ .	....
....	£ .	....
....	£ .	....

TOMORROW'S PLAN

....

....

....

....

....

CAMPER VAN
ROAD TRIP TRAVEL JOURNAL

DATE .... MILEAGE START ....

START TIME .... MILEAGE END ....

ARRIVAL TIME .... MILEAGE TOTAL ....

CAMPSITE NAME OR ....

WILDCAMPING LOCATION ....

ADDRESS 1 ....

ADDRESS 2 ....

GPS .... POST CODE ....

WHAT3WORDS ....

PHONE ....

E MAIL ....

WEBSITE WWW ....

MY RATING .... OUT OF 10   GOOD VALUE - YES / N0

WEATHER .... TEMPERATURE ....

NUMBER OF NIGHTS HERE .... RECOMMEND - YES / NO

DAILY COSTS

SITE FEES   £   .

FUEL   £   .

LPG GAS   £   .

GROCERIES   £   .

EATING OUT   £   .

ENTERTAINMENT   £   .

OTHER COSTS   £   .

.... £   .

.... £   .

TODAY'S HIGHLIGHTS

....

....

....

....

....

....

....

TOMORROW'S PLAN

....

....

....

....

....

CAMPER VAN
ROAD TRIP TRAVEL JOURNAL

DATE .... MILEAGE START ....

START TIME .... MILEAGE END ....

ARRIVAL TIME .... MILEAGE TOTAL ....

CAMPSITE NAME OR ....

WILDCAMPING LOCATION ....

ADDRESS 1 ....

ADDRESS 2 ....

GPS .... POST CODE ....

WHAT3WORDS ....

PHONE ....

E MAIL ....

WEBSITE WWW ....

MY RATING .... OUT OF 10 GOOD VALUE - YES / N0

WEATHER .... TEMPERATURE ....

NUMBER OF NIGHTS HERE .... RECOMMEND - YES / NO

DAILY COSTS	TODAY'S HIGHLIGHTS
SITE FEES £ .	....
FUEL £ .	....
LPG GAS £ .	....
GROCERIES £ .	....
EATING OUT £ .	....
ENTERTAINMENT £ .	....
OTHER COSTS £ .	....
.... £ .	....
.... £ .	....

TOMORROW'S PLAN

....

....

....

....

....

CAMPER VAN
ROAD TRIP TRAVEL JOURNAL

DATE .... MILEAGE START ....

START TIME .... MILEAGE END ....

ARRIVAL TIME .... MILEAGE TOTAL ....

CAMPSITE NAME OR ....

WILDCAMPING LOCATION ....

ADDRESS 1 ....

ADDRESS 2 ....

GPS .... POST CODE ....

WHAT3WORDS ....

PHONE ....

E MAIL ....

WEBSITE WWW ....

MY RATING .... OUT OF 10   GOOD VALUE - YES / N0

WEATHER .... TEMPERATURE ....

NUMBER OF NIGHTS HERE .... RECOMMEND - YES / NO

DAILY COSTS

		TODAY'S HIGHLIGHTS
SITE FEES	£ .	....
FUEL	£ .	....
LPG GAS	£ .	....
GROCERIES	£ .	....
EATING OUT	£ .	....
ENTERTAINMENT	£ .	....
OTHER COSTS	£ .	....
....	£ .	....
....	£ .	....

TOMORROW'S PLAN

....

....

....

....

....

CAMPER VAN
ROAD TRIP TRAVEL JOURNAL

DATE ....   MILEAGE START ....

START TIME ....   MILEAGE END ....

ARRIVAL TIME ....   MILEAGE TOTAL ....

CAMPSITE NAME OR ....

WILDCAMPING LOCATION ....

ADDRESS 1 ....

ADDRESS 2 ....

GPS .... POST CODE ....

WHAT3WORDS ....

PHONE ....

E MAIL ....

WEBSITE WWW ....

MY RATING .... OUT OF 10   GOOD VALUE - YES / N0

WEATHER .... TEMPERATURE ....

NUMBER OF NIGHTS HERE .... RECOMMEND - YES / NO

DAILY COSTS		TODAY'S HIGHLIGHTS
SITE FEES	£ .	....
FUEL	£ .	....
LPG GAS	£ .	....
GROCERIES	£ .	....
EATING OUT	£ .	....
ENTERTAINMENT	£ .	....
OTHER COSTS	£ .	....
....	£ .	....
....	£ .	....

TOMORROW'S PLAN

....

....

....

....

....

CAMPER VAN
ROAD TRIP TRAVEL JOURNAL

DATE ....   MILEAGE START ....

START TIME ....   MILEAGE END ....

ARRIVAL TIME ....   MILEAGE TOTAL ....

CAMPSITE NAME OR ....

WILDCAMPING LOCATION ....

ADDRESS 1 ....

ADDRESS 2 ....

GPS .... POST CODE ....

WHAT3WORDS ....

PHONE ....

E MAIL ....

WEBSITE WWW ....

MY RATING .... OUT OF 10   GOOD VALUE - YES / N0

WEATHER .... TEMPERATURE ....

NUMBER OF NIGHTS HERE .... RECOMMEND - YES / NO

DAILY COSTS		TODAY'S HIGHLIGHTS
SITE FEES	£ .	....
FUEL	£ .	....
LPG GAS	£ .	....
GROCERIES	£ .	....
EATING OUT	£ .	....
ENTERTAINMENT	£ .	....
OTHER COSTS	£ .	....
....	£ .	....
....	£ .	....

TOMORROW'S PLAN

....

....

....

....

....

CAMPER VAN
ROAD TRIP TRAVEL JOURNAL

DATE .... MILEAGE START ....

START TIME .... MILEAGE END ....

ARRIVAL TIME .... MILEAGE TOTAL ....

CAMPSITE NAME OR ....

WILDCAMPING LOCATION ....

ADDRESS 1 ....

ADDRESS 2 ....

GPS .... POST CODE ....

WHAT3WORDS ....

PHONE ....

E MAIL ....

WEBSITE WWW ....

MY RATING .... OUT OF 10   GOOD VALUE - YES / N0

WEATHER .... TEMPERATURE ....

NUMBER OF NIGHTS HERE .... RECOMMEND - YES / NO

DAILY COSTS

SITE FEES   £   .

FUEL   £   .

LPG GAS   £   .

GROCERIES   £   .

EATING OUT   £   .

ENTERTAINMENT   £   .

OTHER COSTS   £   .

.... £   .

.... £   .

TODAY'S HIGHLIGHTS

....

....

....

....

....

....

....

....

TOMORROW'S PLAN

....

....

....

....

....

CAMPER VAN
ROAD TRIP TRAVEL JOURNAL

DATE ....   MILEAGE START ....

START TIME ....   MILEAGE END ....

ARRIVAL TIME ....   MILEAGE TOTAL ....

CAMPSITE NAME OR ....

WILDCAMPING LOCATION ....

ADDRESS 1 ....

ADDRESS 2 ....

GPS .... POST CODE ....

WHAT3WORDS ....

PHONE ....

E MAIL ....

WEBSITE WWW ....

MY RATING .... OUT OF 10   GOOD VALUE - YES / N0

WEATHER .... TEMPERATURE ....

NUMBER OF NIGHTS HERE .... RECOMMEND - YES / NO

DAILY COSTS		TODAY'S HIGHLIGHTS
SITE FEES	£ .	....
FUEL	£ .	....
LPG GAS	£ .	....
GROCERIES	£ .	....
EATING OUT	£ .	....
ENTERTAINMENT	£ .	....
OTHER COSTS	£ .	....
....	£ .	....
....	£ .	....

TOMORROW'S PLAN

....

....

....

....

....

CAMPER VAN
ROAD TRIP TRAVEL JOURNAL

DATE .... MILEAGE START ....

START TIME .... MILEAGE END ....

ARRIVAL TIME .... MILEAGE TOTAL ....

CAMPSITE NAME OR ....

WILDCAMPING LOCATION ....

ADDRESS 1 ....

ADDRESS 2 ....

GPS .... POST CODE ....

WHAT3WORDS ....

PHONE ....

E MAIL ....

WEBSITE WWW ....

MY RATING .... OUT OF 10   GOOD VALUE - YES / N0

WEATHER .... TEMPERATURE ....

NUMBER OF NIGHTS HERE .... RECOMMEND - YES / NO

DAILY COSTS		TODAY'S HIGHLIGHTS
SITE FEES	£ .	....
FUEL	£ .	....
LPG GAS	£ .	....
GROCERIES	£ .	....
EATING OUT	£ .	....
ENTERTAINMENT	£ .	....
OTHER COSTS	£ .	....
....	£ .	....
....	£ .	....

TOMORROW'S PLAN

....

....

....

....

....

CAMPER VAN
ROAD TRIP TRAVEL JOURNAL

DATE .... MILEAGE START ....

START TIME .... MILEAGE END ....

ARRIVAL TIME .... MILEAGE TOTAL ....

CAMPSITE NAME OR ....

WILDCAMPING LOCATION ....

ADDRESS 1 ....

ADDRESS 2 ....

GPS .... POST CODE ....

WHAT3WORDS ....

PHONE ....

E MAIL ....

WEBSITE WWW ....

MY RATING .... OUT OF 10   GOOD VALUE - YES / N0

WEATHER .... TEMPERATURE ....

NUMBER OF NIGHTS HERE .... RECOMMEND - YES / NO

DAILY COSTS

SITE FEES   £   .

FUEL   £   .

LPG GAS   £   .

GROCERIES   £   .

EATING OUT   £   .

ENTERTAINMENT   £   .

OTHER COSTS   £   .

....   £   .

....   £   .

TODAY'S HIGHLIGHTS

....

....

....

....

....

....

....

....

TOMORROW'S PLAN

....

....

....

....

....

CAMPER VAN
ROAD TRIP TRAVEL JOURNAL

DATE .... MILEAGE START ....

START TIME .... MILEAGE END ....

ARRIVAL TIME .... MILEAGE TOTAL ....

CAMPSITE NAME OR ....

WILDCAMPING LOCATION ....

ADDRESS 1 ....

ADDRESS 2 ....

GPS .... POST CODE ....

WHAT3WORDS ....

PHONE ....

E MAIL ....

WEBSITE WWW ....

MY RATING .... OUT OF 10   GOOD VALUE - YES / N0

WEATHER .... TEMPERATURE ....

NUMBER OF NIGHTS HERE .... RECOMMEND - YES / NO

DAILY COSTS		TODAY'S HIGHLIGHTS
SITE FEES	£ .	....
FUEL	£ .	....
LPG GAS	£ .	....
GROCERIES	£ .	....
EATING OUT	£ .	....
ENTERTAINMENT	£ .	....
OTHER COSTS	£ .	....
....	£ .	....
....	£ .	....

TOMORROW'S PLAN

....

....

....

....

....

CAMPER VAN
ROAD TRIP TRAVEL JOURNAL

DATE .... MILEAGE START ....

START TIME .... MILEAGE END ....

ARRIVAL TIME .... MILEAGE TOTAL ....

CAMPSITE NAME OR ....

WILDCAMPING LOCATION ....

ADDRESS 1 ....

ADDRESS 2 ....

GPS .... POST CODE ....

WHAT3WORDS ....

PHONE ....

E MAIL ....

WEBSITE WWW ....

MY RATING .... OUT OF 10   GOOD VALUE - YES / N0

WEATHER .... TEMPERATURE ....

NUMBER OF NIGHTS HERE .... RECOMMEND - YES / NO

DAILY COSTS		TODAY'S HIGHLIGHTS
SITE FEES	£ .	....
FUEL	£ .	....
LPG GAS	£ .	....
GROCERIES	£ .	....
EATING OUT	£ .	....
ENTERTAINMENT	£ .	....
OTHER COSTS	£ .	....
....	£ .	....
....	£ .	....

TOMORROW'S PLAN

....

....

....

....

....

CAMPER VAN
ROAD TRIP TRAVEL JOURNAL

DATE .... MILEAGE START ....

START TIME .... MILEAGE END ....

ARRIVAL TIME .... MILEAGE TOTAL ....

CAMPSITE NAME OR ....

WILDCAMPING LOCATION ....

ADDRESS 1 ....

ADDRESS 2 ....

GPS .... POST CODE ....

WHAT3WORDS ....

PHONE ....

E MAIL ....

WEBSITE WWW ....

MY RATING .... OUT OF 10   GOOD VALUE - YES / N0

WEATHER .... TEMPERATURE ....

NUMBER OF NIGHTS HERE .... RECOMMEND - YES / NO

DAILY COSTS	TODAY'S HIGHLIGHTS
SITE FEES £ .	....
FUEL £ .	....
LPG GAS £ .	....
GROCERIES £ .	....
EATING OUT £ .	....
ENTERTAINMENT £ .	....
OTHER COSTS £ .	....
.... £ .	....
.... £ .	

TOMORROW'S PLAN

....

....

....

....

....

CAMPER VAN
ROAD TRIP TRAVEL JOURNAL

DATE .... MILEAGE START ····················

START TIME .... MILEAGE END ····················

ARRIVAL TIME .... MILEAGE TOTAL ....

CAMPSITE NAME OR ....

WILDCAMPING LOCATION ....

ADDRESS 1 ....

ADDRESS 2 ....

GPS .... POST CODE ....

WHAT3WORDS ....

PHONE ....

E MAIL ....

WEBSITE WWW ....

MY RATING .... OUT OF 10   GOOD VALUE - YES / N0

WEATHER .... TEMPERATURE ....

NUMBER OF NIGHTS HERE .... RECOMMEND - YES / NO

DAILY COSTS		TODAY'S HIGHLIGHTS
SITE FEES	£ .	....
FUEL	£ .	....
LPG GAS	£ .	....
GROCERIES	£ .	....
EATING OUT	£ .	....
ENTERTAINMENT	£ .	....
OTHER COSTS	£ .	....
....	£ .	....
....	£ .	....

TOMORROW'S PLAN

....

....

....

....

....

CAMPER VAN
ROAD TRIP TRAVEL JOURNAL

DATE .... MILEAGE START ....

START TIME .... MILEAGE END ....

ARRIVAL TIME .... MILEAGE TOTAL ....

CAMPSITE NAME OR ....

WILDCAMPING LOCATION ....

ADDRESS 1 ....

ADDRESS 2 ....

GPS .... POST CODE ....

WHAT3WORDS ....

PHONE ....

E MAIL ....

WEBSITE WWW ....

MY RATING .... OUT OF 10   GOOD VALUE - YES / N0

WEATHER .... TEMPERATURE ....

NUMBER OF NIGHTS HERE .... RECOMMEND - YES / NO

DAILY COSTS		TODAY'S HIGHLIGHTS
SITE FEES	£ .	....
FUEL	£ .	....
LPG GAS	£ .	....
GROCERIES	£ .	....
EATING OUT	£ .	....
ENTERTAINMENT	£ .	....
OTHER COSTS	£ .	....
....	£ .	....
....	£ .	....

TOMORROW'S PLAN

....

....

....

....

....

CAMPER VAN
ROAD TRIP TRAVEL JOURNAL

DATE ....   MILEAGE START ....

START TIME ....   MILEAGE END ....

ARRIVAL TIME ....   MILEAGE TOTAL ....

CAMPSITE NAME OR ....

WILDCAMPING LOCATION ....

ADDRESS 1 ....

ADDRESS 2 ....

GPS .... POST CODE ....

WHAT3WORDS ....

PHONE ....

E MAIL ....

WEBSITE WWW ....

MY RATING .... OUT OF 10   GOOD VALUE - YES / N0

WEATHER .... TEMPERATURE ....

NUMBER OF NIGHTS HERE .... RECOMMEND - YES / NO

DAILY COSTS

SITE FEES £ .

FUEL £ .

LPG GAS £ .

GROCERIES £ .

EATING OUT £ .

ENTERTAINMENT £ .

OTHER COSTS £ .

.... £ .

.... £ .

TODAY'S HIGHLIGHTS

....

....

....

....

....

....

....

....

TOMORROW'S PLAN

....

....

....

....

....

CAMPER VAN
ROAD TRIP TRAVEL JOURNAL

DATE .... MILEAGE START ....

START TIME .... MILEAGE END ....

ARRIVAL TIME .... MILEAGE TOTAL ....

CAMPSITE NAME OR ....

WILDCAMPING LOCATION ....

ADDRESS 1 ....

ADDRESS 2 ....

GPS .... POST CODE ....

WHAT3WORDS ....

PHONE ....

E MAIL ....

WEBSITE WWW ....

MY RATING .... OUT OF 10   GOOD VALUE - YES / N0

WEATHER .... TEMPERATURE ....

NUMBER OF NIGHTS HERE .... RECOMMEND - YES / NO

DAILY COSTS		TODAY'S HIGHLIGHTS
SITE FEES	£ .	....
FUEL	£ .	....
LPG GAS	£ .	....
GROCERIES	£ .	....
EATING OUT	£ .	....
ENTERTAINMENT	£ .	....
OTHER COSTS	£ .	....
....	£ .	....
....	£ .	....

TOMORROW'S PLAN

....

....

....

....

....

CAMPER VAN
ROAD TRIP TRAVEL JOURNAL

DATE .... MILEAGE START ....

START TIME .... MILEAGE END ....

ARRIVAL TIME .... MILEAGE TOTAL ....

CAMPSITE NAME OR ....

WILDCAMPING LOCATION ....

ADDRESS 1 ....

ADDRESS 2 ....

GPS .... POST CODE ....

WHAT3WORDS ....

PHONE ....

E MAIL ....

WEBSITE WWW ....

MY RATING .... OUT OF 10   GOOD VALUE - YES / N0

WEATHER .... TEMPERATURE ....

NUMBER OF NIGHTS HERE .... RECOMMEND - YES / NO

DAILY COSTS

SITE FEES £ .

FUEL £ .

LPG GAS £ .

GROCERIES £ .

EATING OUT £ .

ENTERTAINMENT £ .

OTHER COSTS £ .

.... £ .

.... £ .

TODAY'S HIGHLIGHTS

....

....

....

....

....

....

....

TOMORROW'S PLAN

....

....

....

....

....

CAMPER VAN
ROAD TRIP TRAVEL JOURNAL

DATE .... MILEAGE START ....

START TIME .... MILEAGE END ....

ARRIVAL TIME .... MILEAGE TOTAL ....

CAMPSITE NAME OR ....

WILDCAMPING LOCATION ....

ADDRESS 1 ....

ADDRESS 2 ....

GPS .... POST CODE ....

WHAT3WORDS ....

PHONE ....

E MAIL ....

WEBSITE WWW ....

MY RATING .... OUT OF 10   GOOD VALUE - YES / N0

WEATHER .... TEMPERATURE ....

NUMBER OF NIGHTS HERE .... RECOMMEND - YES / NO

DAILY COSTS		TODAY'S HIGHLIGHTS
SITE FEES	£ .	....
FUEL	£ .	....
LPG GAS	£ .	....
GROCERIES	£ .	....
EATING OUT	£ .	....
ENTERTAINMENT	£ .	....
OTHER COSTS	£ .	....
....	£ .	....
....	£ .	

TOMORROW'S PLAN

....

....

....

....

....

CAMPER VAN
ROAD TRIP TRAVEL JOURNAL

DATE .... MILEAGE START ....

START TIME .... MILEAGE END ....

ARRIVAL TIME .... MILEAGE TOTAL ....

CAMPSITE NAME OR ....

WILDCAMPING LOCATION ....

ADDRESS 1 ....

ADDRESS 2 ....

GPS .... POST CODE ....

WHAT3WORDS ....

PHONE ....

E MAIL ....

WEBSITE WWW ....

MY RATING .... OUT OF 10   GOOD VALUE - YES / N0

WEATHER .... TEMPERATURE ....

NUMBER OF NIGHTS HERE .... RECOMMEND - YES / NO

DAILY COSTS

SITE FEES	£ .
FUEL	£ .
LPG GAS	£ .
GROCERIES	£ .
EATING OUT	£ .
ENTERTAINMENT	£ .
OTHER COSTS	£ .
....	£ .
....	£ .

TODAY'S HIGHLIGHTS

....

....

....

....

....

....

....

....

TOMORROW'S PLAN

....

....

....

....

....

CAMPER VAN
ROAD TRIP TRAVEL JOURNAL

DATE .... MILEAGE START ....

START TIME .... MILEAGE END ....

ARRIVAL TIME .... MILEAGE TOTAL ....

CAMPSITE NAME OR ....

WILDCAMPING LOCATION ....

ADDRESS 1 ....

ADDRESS 2 ....

GPS .... POST CODE ....

WHAT3WORDS ....

PHONE ....

E MAIL ....

WEBSITE WWW ....

MY RATING .... OUT OF 10   GOOD VALUE - YES / N0

WEATHER .... TEMPERATURE ....

NUMBER OF NIGHTS HERE .... RECOMMEND - YES / NO

DAILY COSTS		TODAY'S HIGHLIGHTS
SITE FEES	£ .	....
FUEL	£ .	....
LPG GAS	£ .	....
GROCERIES	£ .	....
EATING OUT	£ .	....
ENTERTAINMENT	£ .	....
OTHER COSTS	£ .	....
....	£ .	....
....	£ .	....

TOMORROW'S PLAN

....

....

....

....

....

CAMPER VAN
ROAD TRIP TRAVEL JOURNAL

DATE .... MILEAGE START ....

START TIME .... MILEAGE END ....

ARRIVAL TIME .... MILEAGE TOTAL ....

CAMPSITE NAME OR ....

WILDCAMPING LOCATION ....

ADDRESS 1 ....

ADDRESS 2 ....

GPS .... POST CODE ....

WHAT3WORDS ....

PHONE ....

E MAIL ....

WEBSITE WWW ....

MY RATING .... OUT OF 10   GOOD VALUE - YES / N0

WEATHER .... TEMPERATURE ....

NUMBER OF NIGHTS HERE .... RECOMMEND - YES / NO

DAILY COSTS		TODAY'S HIGHLIGHTS
SITE FEES	£ .	....
FUEL	£ .	....
LPG GAS	£ .	....
GROCERIES	£ .	....
EATING OUT	£ .	....
ENTERTAINMENT	£ .	....
OTHER COSTS	£ .	....
....	£ .	....
....	£ .	....

TOMORROW'S PLAN

....

....

....

....

....

CAMPER VAN
ROAD TRIP TRAVEL JOURNAL

DATE .... MILEAGE START ....

START TIME .... MILEAGE END ....

ARRIVAL TIME .... MILEAGE TOTAL ....

CAMPSITE NAME OR ....

WILDCAMPING LOCATION ....

ADDRESS 1 ....

ADDRESS 2 ....

GPS .... POST CODE ....

WHAT3WORDS ....

PHONE ....

E MAIL ....

WEBSITE WWW ....

MY RATING .... OUT OF 10   GOOD VALUE - YES / N0

WEATHER .... TEMPERATURE ....

NUMBER OF NIGHTS HERE .... RECOMMEND - YES / NO

DAILY COSTS	TODAY'S HIGHLIGHTS
SITE FEES £ .	....
FUEL £ .	....
LPG GAS £ .	....
GROCERIES £ .	....
EATING OUT £ .	....
ENTERTAINMENT £ .	....
OTHER COSTS £ .	....
.... £ .	....
.... £ .	....

TOMORROW'S PLAN

....

....

....

....

....

CAMPER VAN
ROAD TRIP TRAVEL JOURNAL

DATE ....   MILEAGE START ....

START TIME ....   MILEAGE END ....

ARRIVAL TIME ....   MILEAGE TOTAL ....

CAMPSITE NAME OR ....

WILDCAMPING LOCATION ....

ADDRESS 1 ....

ADDRESS 2 ....

GPS .... POST CODE ....

WHAT3WORDS ....

PHONE ....

E MAIL ....

WEBSITE WWW ....

MY RATING .... OUT OF 10   GOOD VALUE - YES / N0

WEATHER .... TEMPERATURE ....

NUMBER OF NIGHTS HERE .... RECOMMEND - YES / NO

DAILY COSTS		TODAY'S HIGHLIGHTS
SITE FEES	£ .	....
FUEL	£ .	....
LPG GAS	£ .	....
GROCERIES	£ .	....
EATING OUT	£ .	....
ENTERTAINMENT	£ .	....
OTHER COSTS	£ .	....
....	£ .	....
....	£ .	....

TOMORROW'S PLAN

....

....

....

....

....

CAMPER VAN
ROAD TRIP TRAVEL JOURNAL

DATE .... MILEAGE START ....

START TIME .... MILEAGE END ....

ARRIVAL TIME .... MILEAGE TOTAL ....

CAMPSITE NAME OR ....

WILDCAMPING LOCATION ....

ADDRESS 1 ....

ADDRESS 2 ....

GPS .... POST CODE ....

WHAT3WORDS ....

PHONE ....

E MAIL ....

WEBSITE WWW ....

MY RATING .... OUT OF 10   GOOD VALUE - YES / N0

WEATHER .... TEMPERATURE ....

NUMBER OF NIGHTS HERE .... RECOMMEND - YES / NO

DAILY COSTS		TODAY'S HIGHLIGHTS
SITE FEES	£ .	....
FUEL	£ .	....
LPG GAS	£ .	....
GROCERIES	£ .	....
EATING OUT	£ .	....
ENTERTAINMENT	£ .	....
OTHER COSTS	£ .	....
....	£ .	....
....	£ .	....

TOMORROW'S PLAN

....

....

....

....

....

CAMPER VAN
ROAD TRIP TRAVEL JOURNAL

DATE ....   MILEAGE START ....

START TIME ....   MILEAGE END ....

ARRIVAL TIME ....   MILEAGE TOTAL ....

CAMPSITE NAME OR ....

WILDCAMPING LOCATION ....

ADDRESS 1 ....

ADDRESS 2 ....

GPS .... POST CODE ....

WHAT3WORDS ....

PHONE ....

E MAIL ....

WEBSITE WWW ....

MY RATING .... OUT OF 10   GOOD VALUE - YES / N0

WEATHER .... TEMPERATURE ....

NUMBER OF NIGHTS HERE .... RECOMMEND - YES / NO

DAILY COSTS		TODAY'S HIGHLIGHTS
SITE FEES	£ .	....
FUEL	£ .	....
LPG GAS	£ .	....
GROCERIES	£ .	....
EATING OUT	£ .	....
ENTERTAINMENT	£ .	....
OTHER COSTS	£ .	....
....	£ .	....
....	£ .	....

TOMORROW'S PLAN

....

....

....

....

....

CAMPER VAN
ROAD TRIP TRAVEL JOURNAL

DATE .... MILEAGE START ....

START TIME .... MILEAGE END ....

ARRIVAL TIME .... MILEAGE TOTAL ....

CAMPSITE NAME OR ....

WILDCAMPING LOCATION ....

ADDRESS 1 ....

ADDRESS 2 ....

GPS .... POST CODE ....

WHAT3WORDS ....

PHONE ....

E MAIL ....

WEBSITE WWW ....

MY RATING .... OUT OF 10   GOOD VALUE - YES / N0

WEATHER .... TEMPERATURE ....

NUMBER OF NIGHTS HERE .... RECOMMEND - YES / NO

DAILY COSTS		TODAY'S HIGHLIGHTS
SITE FEES	£ .	....
FUEL	£ .	....
LPG GAS	£ .	....
GROCERIES	£ .	....
EATING OUT	£ .	....
ENTERTAINMENT	£ .	....
OTHER COSTS	£ .	....
....	£ .	....
....	£ .	....

TOMORROW'S PLAN

....

....

....

....

....

CAMPER VAN
ROAD TRIP TRAVEL JOURNAL

DATE .... MILEAGE START ....

START TIME .... MILEAGE END ....

ARRIVAL TIME .... MILEAGE TOTAL ....

CAMPSITE NAME OR ....

WILDCAMPING LOCATION ....

ADDRESS 1 ....

ADDRESS 2 ....

GPS .... POST CODE ....

WHAT3WORDS ....

PHONE ....

E MAIL ....

WEBSITE WWW ....

MY RATING .... OUT OF 10   GOOD VALUE - YES / N0

WEATHER .... TEMPERATURE ....

NUMBER OF NIGHTS HERE .... RECOMMEND - YES / NO

DAILY COSTS		TODAY'S HIGHLIGHTS
SITE FEES	£ .	....
FUEL	£ .	....
LPG GAS	£ .	....
GROCERIES	£ .	....
EATING OUT	£ .	....
ENTERTAINMENT	£ .	....
OTHER COSTS	£ .	....
....	£ .	....
....	£ .	....

TOMORROW'S PLAN

....

....

....

....

....

CAMPER VAN
ROAD TRIP TRAVEL JOURNAL

DATE .... MILEAGE START ....

START TIME .... MILEAGE END ....

ARRIVAL TIME .... MILEAGE TOTAL ....

CAMPSITE NAME OR ....

WILDCAMPING LOCATION ....

ADDRESS 1 ....

ADDRESS 2 ....

GPS .... POST CODE ....

WHAT3WORDS ....

PHONE ....

E MAIL ....

WEBSITE WWW ....

MY RATING .... OUT OF 10   GOOD VALUE - YES / N0

WEATHER .... TEMPERATURE ....

NUMBER OF NIGHTS HERE .... RECOMMEND - YES / NO

DAILY COSTS		TODAY'S HIGHLIGHTS
SITE FEES	£ .	....
FUEL	£ .	....
LPG GAS	£ .	....
GROCERIES	£ .	....
EATING OUT	£ .	....
ENTERTAINMENT	£ .	....
OTHER COSTS	£ .	....
....	£ .	....
....	£ .	....

TOMORROW'S PLAN

....

....

....

....

....

CAMPER VAN
ROAD TRIP TRAVEL JOURNAL

DATE .... MILEAGE START ....

START TIME .... MILEAGE END ....

ARRIVAL TIME .... MILEAGE TOTAL ....

CAMPSITE NAME OR ....

WILDCAMPING LOCATION ....

ADDRESS 1 ....

ADDRESS 2 ....

GPS .... POST CODE ....

WHAT3WORDS ....

PHONE ....

E MAIL ....

WEBSITE WWW ....

MY RATING .... OUT OF 10   GOOD VALUE - YES / N0

WEATHER .... TEMPERATURE ....

NUMBER OF NIGHTS HERE .... RECOMMEND - YES / NO

DAILY COSTS

SITE FEES	£ .
FUEL	£ .
LPG GAS	£ .
GROCERIES	£ .
EATING OUT	£ .
ENTERTAINMENT	£ .
OTHER COSTS	£ .
....	£ .
....	£ .

TODAY'S HIGHLIGHTS

....

....

....

....

....

....

....

....

TOMORROW'S PLAN

....

....

....

....

....

CAMPER VAN
ROAD TRIP TRAVEL JOURNAL

DATE .... MILEAGE START ....

START TIME .... MILEAGE END ....

ARRIVAL TIME .... MILEAGE TOTAL ....

CAMPSITE NAME OR ....

WILDCAMPING LOCATION ....

ADDRESS 1 ....

ADDRESS 2 ....

GPS .... POST CODE ....

WHAT3WORDS ....

PHONE ....

E MAIL ....

WEBSITE WWW ....

MY RATING .... OUT OF 10   GOOD VALUE - YES / NO

WEATHER .... TEMPERATURE ....

NUMBER OF NIGHTS HERE .... RECOMMEND - YES / NO

DAILY COSTS

SITE FEES   £   .

FUEL   £   .

LPG GAS
                 £   .
GROCERIES
                 £   .
EATING OUT
                 £   .
ENTERTAINMENT
                 £   .
OTHER COSTS
                 £   .
....   £   .

....   £   .

TODAY'S HIGHLIGHTS

....

....

....

....

....

....

....

TOMORROW'S PLAN

....

....

....

....

....

CAMPER VAN
ROAD TRIP TRAVEL JOURNAL

DATE .... MILEAGE START ....

START TIME .... MILEAGE END ....

ARRIVAL TIME .... MILEAGE TOTAL ....

CAMPSITE NAME OR ....

WILDCAMPING LOCATION ....

ADDRESS 1 ....

ADDRESS 2 ....

GPS .... POST CODE ....

WHAT3WORDS ....

PHONE ....

E MAIL ....

WEBSITE WWW ....

MY RATING .... OUT OF 10   GOOD VALUE - YES / N0

WEATHER .... TEMPERATURE ....

NUMBER OF NIGHTS HERE .... RECOMMEND - YES / NO

DAILY COSTS		TODAY'S HIGHLIGHTS
SITE FEES	£ .	....
FUEL	£ .	....
LPG GAS	£ .	....
GROCERIES	£ .	....
EATING OUT	£ .	....
ENTERTAINMENT	£ .	....
OTHER COSTS	£ .	....
....	£ .	....
....	£ .	....

TOMORROW'S PLAN

....

....

....

....

....

CAMPER VAN
ROAD TRIP TRAVEL JOURNAL

DATE .... MILEAGE START ....

START TIME .... MILEAGE END ....

ARRIVAL TIME .... MILEAGE TOTAL ....

CAMPSITE NAME OR ....

WILDCAMPING LOCATION ....

ADDRESS 1 ....

ADDRESS 2 ....

GPS .... POST CODE ....

WHAT3WORDS ....

PHONE ....

E MAIL ....

WEBSITE WWW ....

MY RATING .... OUT OF 10   GOOD VALUE - YES / N0

WEATHER .... TEMPERATURE ....

NUMBER OF NIGHTS HERE .... RECOMMEND - YES / NO

DAILY COSTS		TODAY'S HIGHLIGHTS
SITE FEES	£ .	....
FUEL	£ .	....
LPG GAS	£ .	....
GROCERIES	£ .	....
EATING OUT	£ .	....
ENTERTAINMENT	£ .	....
OTHER COSTS	£ .	....
....	£ .	....
....	£ .	....

TOMORROW'S PLAN

....

....

....

....

....

CAMPER VAN
ROAD TRIP TRAVEL JOURNAL

DATE .... MILEAGE START ....

START TIME .... MILEAGE END ....

ARRIVAL TIME .... MILEAGE TOTAL ....

CAMPSITE NAME OR ....

WILDCAMPING LOCATION ....

ADDRESS 1 ....

ADDRESS 2 ....

GPS .... POST CODE ....

WHAT3WORDS ....

PHONE ....

E MAIL ....

WEBSITE WWW ....

MY RATING .... OUT OF 10   GOOD VALUE - YES / N0

WEATHER .... TEMPERATURE ....

NUMBER OF NIGHTS HERE .... RECOMMEND - YES / NO

DAILY COSTS

SITE FEES	£ .
FUEL	£ .
LPG GAS	£ .
GROCERIES	£ .
EATING OUT	£ .
ENTERTAINMENT	£ .
OTHER COSTS	£ .
....	£ .
....	£ .

TODAY'S HIGHLIGHTS

....

....

....

....

....

....

....

TOMORROW'S PLAN

....

....

....

....

....

CAMPER VAN
ROAD TRIP TRAVEL JOURNAL

DATE .... MILEAGE START ....

START TIME .... MILEAGE END ....

ARRIVAL TIME .... MILEAGE TOTAL ....

CAMPSITE NAME OR ....

WILDCAMPING LOCATION ....

ADDRESS 1 ....

ADDRESS 2 ....

GPS .... POST CODE ....

WHAT3WORDS ....

PHONE ....

E MAIL ....

WEBSITE WWW ....

MY RATING .... OUT OF 10   GOOD VALUE - YES / NO

WEATHER .... TEMPERATURE ....

NUMBER OF NIGHTS HERE .... RECOMMEND - YES / NO

DAILY COSTS	TODAY'S HIGHLIGHTS
SITE FEES £ .	....
FUEL £ .	....
LPG GAS £ .	....
GROCERIES £ .	....
EATING OUT £ .	....
ENTERTAINMENT £ .	....
OTHER COSTS £ .	....
.... £ .	....
.... £ .	....

TOMORROW'S PLAN

....

....

....

....

....

CAMPER VAN
ROAD TRIP TRAVEL JOURNAL

DATE .... MILEAGE START ....

START TIME .... MILEAGE END ....

ARRIVAL TIME .... MILEAGE TOTAL ....

CAMPSITE NAME OR ....

WILDCAMPING LOCATION ....

ADDRESS 1 ....

ADDRESS 2 ....

GPS .... POST CODE ....

WHAT3WORDS ....

PHONE ....

E MAIL ....

WEBSITE WWW ....

MY RATING .... OUT OF 10   GOOD VALUE - YES / N0

WEATHER .... TEMPERATURE ....

NUMBER OF NIGHTS HERE .... RECOMMEND - YES / NO

DAILY COSTS		TODAY'S HIGHLIGHTS
SITE FEES	£ .	....
FUEL	£ .	....
LPG GAS	£ .	....
GROCERIES	£ .	....
EATING OUT	£ .	....
ENTERTAINMENT	£ .	....
OTHER COSTS	£ .	....
....	£ .	....
....	£ .	....

TOMORROW'S PLAN

....

....

....

....

....

CAMPER VAN
ROAD TRIP TRAVEL JOURNAL

DATE .... MILEAGE START ....

START TIME .... MILEAGE END ....

ARRIVAL TIME .... MILEAGE TOTAL ....

CAMPSITE NAME OR ....

WILDCAMPING LOCATION ....

ADDRESS 1 ....

ADDRESS 2 ....

GPS .... POST CODE ....

WHAT3WORDS ....

PHONE ....

E MAIL ....

WEBSITE WWW ....

MY RATING .... OUT OF 10   GOOD VALUE - YES / N0

WEATHER .... TEMPERATURE ....

NUMBER OF NIGHTS HERE .... RECOMMEND - YES / NO

DAILY COSTS		TODAY'S HIGHLIGHTS
SITE FEES	£ .	....
FUEL	£ .	....
LPG GAS	£ .	....
GROCERIES	£ .	....
EATING OUT	£ .	....
ENTERTAINMENT	£ .	....
OTHER COSTS	£ .	....
....	£ .	....
....	£ .	....

TOMORROW'S PLAN

....

....

....

....

....

CAMPER VAN
ROAD TRIP TRAVEL JOURNAL

DATE .... MILEAGE START ....

START TIME .... MILEAGE END ....

ARRIVAL TIME .... MILEAGE TOTAL ....

CAMPSITE NAME OR ....

WILDCAMPING LOCATION ....

ADDRESS 1 ....

ADDRESS 2 ....

GPS .... POST CODE ....

WHAT3WORDS ....

PHONE ....

E MAIL ....

WEBSITE WWW ....

MY RATING .... OUT OF 10   GOOD VALUE - YES / N0

WEATHER .... TEMPERATURE ....

NUMBER OF NIGHTS HERE .... RECOMMEND - YES / NO

DAILY COSTS		TODAY'S HIGHLIGHTS
SITE FEES	£ .	....
FUEL	£ .	....
LPG GAS	£ .	....
GROCERIES	£ .	....
EATING OUT	£ .	....
ENTERTAINMENT	£ .	....
OTHER COSTS	£ .	....
....	£ .	....
....	£ .	....

TOMORROW'S PLAN

....

....

....

....

....

CAMPER VAN
ROAD TRIP TRAVEL JOURNAL

DATE .... MILEAGE START ....

START TIME .... MILEAGE END ....

ARRIVAL TIME .... MILEAGE TOTAL ....

CAMPSITE NAME OR ....

WILDCAMPING LOCATION ....

ADDRESS 1 ....

ADDRESS 2 ....

GPS .... POST CODE ....

WHAT3WORDS ....

PHONE ....

E MAIL ....

WEBSITE WWW ....

MY RATING .... OUT OF 10   GOOD VALUE - YES / N0

WEATHER .... TEMPERATURE ....

NUMBER OF NIGHTS HERE .... RECOMMEND - YES / NO

DAILY COSTS	TODAY'S HIGHLIGHTS
SITE FEES £ .	....
FUEL £ .	....
LPG GAS £ .	....
GROCERIES £ .	....
EATING OUT £ .	....
ENTERTAINMENT £ .	....
OTHER COSTS £ .	....
.... £ .	....
.... £ .	....

TOMORROW'S PLAN

....

....

....

....

....

CAMPER VAN
ROAD TRIP TRAVEL JOURNAL

DATE .... MILEAGE START ....

START TIME .... MILEAGE END ....

ARRIVAL TIME .... MILEAGE TOTAL ....

CAMPSITE NAME OR ....

WILDCAMPING LOCATION ....

ADDRESS 1 ....

ADDRESS 2 ....

GPS .... POST CODE ....

WHAT3WORDS ....

PHONE ....

E MAIL ....

WEBSITE WWW ....

MY RATING .... OUT OF 10   GOOD VALUE - YES / N0

WEATHER .... TEMPERATURE ....

NUMBER OF NIGHTS HERE .... RECOMMEND - YES / NO

DAILY COSTS

		TODAY'S HIGHLIGHTS
SITE FEES	£ .	....
FUEL	£ .	....
LPG GAS	£ .	....
GROCERIES	£ .	....
EATING OUT	£ .	....
ENTERTAINMENT	£ .	....
OTHER COSTS	£ .	....
....	£ .	....
....	£ .	....

TOMORROW'S PLAN

....

....

....

....

....

CAMPER VAN
ROAD TRIP TRAVEL JOURNAL

DATE .... MILEAGE START ....

START TIME .... MILEAGE END ....

ARRIVAL TIME .... MILEAGE TOTAL ....

CAMPSITE NAME OR ....

WILDCAMPING LOCATION ....

ADDRESS 1 ....

ADDRESS 2 ....

GPS .... POST CODE ....

WHAT3WORDS ....

PHONE ....

E MAIL ....

WEBSITE WWW ....

MY RATING .... OUT OF 10   GOOD VALUE - YES / N0

WEATHER .... TEMPERATURE ....

NUMBER OF NIGHTS HERE .... RECOMMEND - YES / NO

DAILY COSTS		TODAY'S HIGHLIGHTS
SITE FEES	£ .	....
FUEL	£ .	....
LPG GAS	£ .	....
GROCERIES	£ .	....
EATING OUT	£ .	....
ENTERTAINMENT	£ .	....
OTHER COSTS	£ .	....
....	£ .	....
....	£ .	....

TOMORROW'S PLAN

....

....

....

....

....

CAMPER VAN
ROAD TRIP TRAVEL JOURNAL

DATE .... MILEAGE START ....

START TIME .... MILEAGE END ....

ARRIVAL TIME .... MILEAGE TOTAL ....

CAMPSITE NAME OR ....

WILDCAMPING LOCATION ....

ADDRESS 1 ....

ADDRESS 2 ....

GPS .... POST CODE ....

WHAT3WORDS ....

PHONE ....

E MAIL ....

WEBSITE WWW ....

MY RATING .... OUT OF 10   GOOD VALUE - YES / N0

WEATHER .... TEMPERATURE ....

NUMBER OF NIGHTS HERE .... RECOMMEND - YES / NO

DAILY COSTS	TODAY'S HIGHLIGHTS
SITE FEES £ .	....
FUEL £ .	....
LPG GAS £ .	....
GROCERIES £ .	....
EATING OUT £ .	....
ENTERTAINMENT £ .	....
OTHER COSTS £ .	....
.... £ .	....
.... £ .	....

TOMORROW'S PLAN

....

....

....

....

....

CAMPER VAN
ROAD TRIP TRAVEL JOURNAL

DATE .... MILEAGE START ....

START TIME .... MILEAGE END ....

ARRIVAL TIME .... MILEAGE TOTAL ....

CAMPSITE NAME OR ....

WILDCAMPING LOCATION ....

ADDRESS 1 ....

ADDRESS 2 ....

GPS .... POST CODE ....

WHAT3WORDS ....

PHONE ....

E MAIL ....

WEBSITE WWW ....

MY RATING .... OUT OF 10   GOOD VALUE - YES / N0

WEATHER .... TEMPERATURE ....

NUMBER OF NIGHTS HERE .... RECOMMEND - YES / NO

DAILY COSTS

SITE FEES £ .

FUEL £ .

LPG GAS £ .

GROCERIES £ .

EATING OUT £ .

ENTERTAINMENT £ .

OTHER COSTS £ .

.... £ .

.... £ .

TODAY'S HIGHLIGHTS

....

....

....

....

....

....

....

....

TOMORROW'S PLAN

....

....

....

....

....

CAMPER VAN
ROAD TRIP TRAVEL JOURNAL

DATE ....   MILEAGE START ....

START TIME ....   MILEAGE END ....

ARRIVAL TIME ....   MILEAGE TOTAL ....

CAMPSITE NAME OR ....

WILDCAMPING LOCATION ....

ADDRESS 1 ....

ADDRESS 2 ....

GPS .... POST CODE ....

WHAT3WORDS ....

PHONE ....

E MAIL ....

WEBSITE WWW ....

MY RATING .... OUT OF 10   GOOD VALUE - YES / N0

WEATHER .... TEMPERATURE ....

NUMBER OF NIGHTS HERE .... RECOMMEND - YES / NO

DAILY COSTS		TODAY'S HIGHLIGHTS
SITE FEES	£ .	....
FUEL	£ .	....
LPG GAS	£ .	....
GROCERIES	£ .	....
EATING OUT	£ .	....
ENTERTAINMENT	£ .	....
OTHER COSTS	£ .	....
....	£ .	....
....	£ .	....

TOMORROW'S PLAN

....

....

....

....

....

CAMPER VAN
ROAD TRIP TRAVEL JOURNAL

DATE .... MILEAGE START ....

START TIME .... MILEAGE END ....

ARRIVAL TIME .... MILEAGE TOTAL ....

CAMPSITE NAME OR ....

WILDCAMPING LOCATION ....

ADDRESS 1 ....

ADDRESS 2 ....

GPS .... POST CODE ....

WHAT3WORDS ....

PHONE ....

E MAIL ....

WEBSITE WWW ....

MY RATING .... OUT OF 10   GOOD VALUE - YES / N0

WEATHER .... TEMPERATURE ....

NUMBER OF NIGHTS HERE .... RECOMMEND - YES / NO

DAILY COSTS		TODAY'S HIGHLIGHTS
SITE FEES	£ .	....
FUEL	£ .	....
LPG GAS	£ .	....
GROCERIES	£ .	....
EATING OUT	£ .	....
ENTERTAINMENT	£ .	....
OTHER COSTS	£ .	....
....	£ .	....
....	£ .	....

TOMORROW'S PLAN

....

....

....

....

....

CAMPER VAN
ROAD TRIP TRAVEL JOURNAL

DATE .... MILEAGE START ....

START TIME .... MILEAGE END ....

ARRIVAL TIME .... MILEAGE TOTAL ....

CAMPSITE NAME OR ....

WILDCAMPING LOCATION ....

ADDRESS 1 ....

ADDRESS 2 ....

GPS .... POST CODE ....

WHAT3WORDS ....

PHONE ....

E MAIL ....

WEBSITE WWW ....

MY RATING .... OUT OF 10   GOOD VALUE - YES / N0

WEATHER .... TEMPERATURE ....

NUMBER OF NIGHTS HERE .... RECOMMEND - YES / NO

DAILY COSTS		TODAY'S HIGHLIGHTS
SITE FEES	£ .	....
FUEL	£ .	....
LPG GAS	£ .	....
GROCERIES	£ .	....
EATING OUT	£ .	....
ENTERTAINMENT	£ .	....
OTHER COSTS	£ .	....
....	£ .	....
....	£ .	....

TOMORROW'S PLAN

....

....

....

....

....

CAMPER VAN
ROAD TRIP TRAVEL JOURNAL

DATE .... MILEAGE START ....

START TIME .... MILEAGE END ....

ARRIVAL TIME .... MILEAGE TOTAL ....

CAMPSITE NAME OR ....

WILDCAMPING LOCATION ....

ADDRESS 1 ....

ADDRESS 2 ....

GPS .... POST CODE ....

WHAT3WORDS ....

PHONE ....

E MAIL ....

WEBSITE WWW ....

MY RATING .... OUT OF 10   GOOD VALUE - YES / N0

WEATHER .... TEMPERATURE ....

NUMBER OF NIGHTS HERE .... RECOMMEND - YES / NO

DAILY COSTS

		TODAY'S HIGHLIGHTS
SITE FEES	£ .	....
FUEL	£ .	....
LPG GAS	£ .	....
GROCERIES	£ .	....
EATING OUT	£ .	....
ENTERTAINMENT	£ .	....
OTHER COSTS	£ .	....
....	£ .	....
....	£ .	....

TOMORROW'S PLAN

....

....

....

....

....

CAMPER VAN
ROAD TRIP TRAVEL JOURNAL

DATE .... MILEAGE START ....

START TIME .... MILEAGE END ....

ARRIVAL TIME .... MILEAGE TOTAL ....

CAMPSITE NAME OR ....

WILDCAMPING LOCATION ....

ADDRESS 1 ....

ADDRESS 2 ....

GPS .... POST CODE ....

WHAT3WORDS ....

PHONE ....

E MAIL ....

WEBSITE WWW ....

MY RATING .... OUT OF 10 GOOD VALUE - YES / N0

WEATHER .... TEMPERATURE ....

NUMBER OF NIGHTS HERE .... RECOMMEND - YES / NO

DAILY COSTS		TODAY'S HIGHLIGHTS
SITE FEES	£ .	....
FUEL	£ .	....
LPG GAS	£ .	....
GROCERIES	£ .	....
EATING OUT	£ .	....
ENTERTAINMENT	£ .	....
OTHER COSTS	£ .	....
....	£ .	....
....	£ .	....

TOMORROW'S PLAN

....

....

....

....

....

CAMPER VAN
ROAD TRIP TRAVEL JOURNAL

DATE .... MILEAGE START ....

START TIME .... MILEAGE END ....

ARRIVAL TIME .... MILEAGE TOTAL ....

CAMPSITE NAME OR ....

WILDCAMPING LOCATION ....

ADDRESS 1 ....

ADDRESS 2 ....

GPS .... POST CODE ....

WHAT3WORDS ....

PHONE ....

E MAIL ....

WEBSITE WWW ....

MY RATING .... OUT OF 10   GOOD VALUE - YES / N0

WEATHER .... TEMPERATURE ....

NUMBER OF NIGHTS HERE .... RECOMMEND - YES / NO

DAILY COSTS		TODAY'S HIGHLIGHTS
SITE FEES	£ .	....
FUEL	£ .	....
LPG GAS	£ .	....
GROCERIES	£ .	....
EATING OUT	£ .	....
ENTERTAINMENT	£ .	....
OTHER COSTS	£ .	....
....	£ .	....
....	£ .	....

TOMORROW'S PLAN

....

....

....

....

....

CAMPER VAN
ROAD TRIP TRAVEL JOURNAL

DATE .... MILEAGE START ....

START TIME .... MILEAGE END ....

ARRIVAL TIME .... MILEAGE TOTAL ....

CAMPSITE NAME OR ....

WILDCAMPING LOCATION ....

ADDRESS 1 ....

ADDRESS 2 ....

GPS .... POST CODE ....

WHAT3WORDS ....

PHONE ....

E MAIL ....

WEBSITE WWW ....

MY RATING .... OUT OF 10   GOOD VALUE - YES / N0

WEATHER .... TEMPERATURE ....

NUMBER OF NIGHTS HERE .... RECOMMEND - YES / NO

DAILY COSTS

SITE FEES   £   .

FUEL   £   .

LPG GAS   £   .

GROCERIES   £   .

EATING OUT   £   .

ENTERTAINMENT   £   .

OTHER COSTS   £   .

....   £   .

....   £   .

TODAY'S HIGHLIGHTS

....
....
....
....
....
....
....
....

TOMORROW'S PLAN

....
....
....
....
....

CAMPER VAN
ROAD TRIP TRAVEL JOURNAL

DATE .... MILEAGE START ....

START TIME .... MILEAGE END ....

ARRIVAL TIME .... MILEAGE TOTAL ....

CAMPSITE NAME OR ....

WILDCAMPING LOCATION ....

ADDRESS 1 ....

ADDRESS 2 ....

GPS .... POST CODE ....

WHAT3WORDS ....

PHONE ....

E MAIL ....

WEBSITE WWW ....

MY RATING .... OUT OF 10   GOOD VALUE - YES / N0

WEATHER .... TEMPERATURE ....

NUMBER OF NIGHTS HERE .... RECOMMEND - YES / NO

DAILY COSTS		TODAY'S HIGHLIGHTS
SITE FEES	£ .	....
FUEL	£ .	....
LPG GAS	£ .	....
GROCERIES	£ .	....
EATING OUT	£ .	....
ENTERTAINMENT	£ .	....
OTHER COSTS	£ .	....
....	£ .	....
....	£ .	....

TOMORROW'S PLAN

....

....

....

....

....

CAMPER VAN
ROAD TRIP TRAVEL JOURNAL

DATE .... MILEAGE START ....

START TIME .... MILEAGE END ....

ARRIVAL TIME .... MILEAGE TOTAL ....

CAMPSITE NAME OR ....

WILDCAMPING LOCATION ....

ADDRESS 1 ....

ADDRESS 2 ....

GPS .... POST CODE ....

WHAT3WORDS ....

PHONE ....

E MAIL ....

WEBSITE WWW ....

MY RATING .... OUT OF 10   GOOD VALUE - YES / N0

WEATHER .... TEMPERATURE ....

NUMBER OF NIGHTS HERE .... RECOMMEND - YES / NO

DAILY COSTS	TODAY'S HIGHLIGHTS
SITE FEES £ .	....
FUEL £ .	....
LPG GAS £ .	....
GROCERIES £ .	....
EATING OUT £ .	....
ENTERTAINMENT £ .	....
OTHER COSTS £ .	....
.... £ .	....
.... £ .	....

TOMORROW'S PLAN

....

....

....

....

....

CAMPER VAN
ROAD TRIP TRAVEL JOURNAL

DATE .... MILEAGE START ....

START TIME .... MILEAGE END ....

ARRIVAL TIME .... MILEAGE TOTAL ....

CAMPSITE NAME OR ....

WILDCAMPING LOCATION ....

ADDRESS 1 ....

ADDRESS 2 ....

GPS .... POST CODE ....

WHAT3WORDS ....

PHONE ....

E MAIL ....

WEBSITE WWW ....

MY RATING .... OUT OF 10   GOOD VALUE - YES / N0

WEATHER .... TEMPERATURE ....

NUMBER OF NIGHTS HERE .... RECOMMEND - YES / NO

DAILY COSTS		TODAY'S HIGHLIGHTS
SITE FEES	£ .	....
FUEL	£ .	....
LPG GAS	£ .	....
GROCERIES	£ .	....
EATING OUT	£ .	....
ENTERTAINMENT	£ .	....
OTHER COSTS	£ .	....
....	£ .	....
....	£ .	....

TOMORROW'S PLAN

....

....

....

....

....

CAMPER VAN
ROAD TRIP TRAVEL JOURNAL

DATE ....   MILEAGE START ....

START TIME ....   MILEAGE END ....

ARRIVAL TIME ....   MILEAGE TOTAL ....

CAMPSITE NAME OR ....

WILDCAMPING LOCATION ....

ADDRESS 1 ....

ADDRESS 2 ....

GPS .... POST CODE ....

WHAT3WORDS ....

PHONE ....

E MAIL ....

WEBSITE WWW ....

MY RATING .... OUT OF 10   GOOD VALUE - YES / N0

WEATHER .... TEMPERATURE ....

NUMBER OF NIGHTS HERE .... RECOMMEND - YES / NO

DAILY COSTS		TODAY'S HIGHLIGHTS
SITE FEES	£ .	....
FUEL	£ .	....
LPG GAS	£ .	....
GROCERIES	£ .	....
EATING OUT	£ .	....
ENTERTAINMENT	£ .	....
OTHER COSTS	£ .	....
....	£ .	....
....	£ .	....

TOMORROW'S PLAN

....

....

....

....

....

CAMPER VAN
ROAD TRIP TRAVEL JOURNAL

DATE .... MILEAGE START ....

START TIME .... MILEAGE END ....

ARRIVAL TIME .... MILEAGE TOTAL ....

CAMPSITE NAME OR ....

WILDCAMPING LOCATION ....

ADDRESS 1 ....

ADDRESS 2 ....

GPS .... POST CODE ....

WHAT3WORDS ....

PHONE ....

E MAIL ....

WEBSITE WWW ....

MY RATING .... OUT OF 10   GOOD VALUE - YES / N0

WEATHER .... TEMPERATURE ....

NUMBER OF NIGHTS HERE .... RECOMMEND - YES / NO

DAILY COSTS	TODAY'S HIGHLIGHTS
SITE FEES £ .	....
FUEL £ .	....
LPG GAS £ .	....
GROCERIES £ .	....
EATING OUT £ .	....
ENTERTAINMENT £ .	....
OTHER COSTS £ .	....
.... £ .	....
.... £ .	....

TOMORROW'S PLAN

....

....

....

....

....

CAMPER VAN
ROAD TRIP TRAVEL JOURNAL

DATE .... MILEAGE START ....

START TIME .... MILEAGE END ....

ARRIVAL TIME .... MILEAGE TOTAL ....

CAMPSITE NAME OR ....

WILDCAMPING LOCATION ....

ADDRESS 1 ....

ADDRESS 2 ....

GPS .... POST CODE ....

WHAT3WORDS ....

PHONE ....

E MAIL ....

WEBSITE WWW ....

MY RATING .... OUT OF 10   GOOD VALUE - YES / N0

WEATHER .... TEMPERATURE ....

NUMBER OF NIGHTS HERE .... RECOMMEND - YES / NO

DAILY COSTS		TODAY'S HIGHLIGHTS
SITE FEES	£ .	....
FUEL	£ .	....
LPG GAS	£ .	....
GROCERIES	£ .	....
EATING OUT	£ .	....
ENTERTAINMENT	£ .	....
OTHER COSTS	£ .	....
....	£ .	....
....	£ .	....

TOMORROW'S PLAN

....

....

....

....

....

CAMPER VAN
ROAD TRIP TRAVEL JOURNAL

DATE .... MILEAGE START ....

START TIME .... MILEAGE END ....

ARRIVAL TIME .... MILEAGE TOTAL ....

CAMPSITE NAME OR ....

WILDCAMPING LOCATION ....

ADDRESS 1 ....

ADDRESS 2 ....

GPS .... POST CODE ....

WHAT3WORDS ....

PHONE ....

E MAIL ....

WEBSITE WWW ....

MY RATING .... OUT OF 10   GOOD VALUE - YES / N0

WEATHER .... TEMPERATURE ....

NUMBER OF NIGHTS HERE .... RECOMMEND - YES / NO

DAILY COSTS		TODAY'S HIGHLIGHTS
SITE FEES	£ .	....
FUEL	£ .	....
LPG GAS	£ .	....
GROCERIES	£ .	....
EATING OUT	£ .	....
ENTERTAINMENT	£ .	....
OTHER COSTS	£ .	....
....	£ .	....
....	£ .	....

TOMORROW'S PLAN

....

....

....

....

....

CAMPER VAN
ROAD TRIP TRAVEL JOURNAL

DATE .... MILEAGE START ....

START TIME .... MILEAGE END ....

ARRIVAL TIME .... MILEAGE TOTAL ....

CAMPSITE NAME OR ....

WILDCAMPING LOCATION ....

ADDRESS 1 ....

ADDRESS 2 ....

GPS .... POST CODE ....

WHAT3WORDS ....

PHONE ....

E MAIL ....

WEBSITE WWW ....

MY RATING .... OUT OF 10   GOOD VALUE - YES / N0

WEATHER .... TEMPERATURE ....

NUMBER OF NIGHTS HERE .... RECOMMEND - YES / NO

DAILY COSTS		TODAY'S HIGHLIGHTS
SITE FEES	£ .	....
FUEL	£ .	....
LPG GAS	£ .	....
GROCERIES	£ .	....
EATING OUT	£ .	....
ENTERTAINMENT	£ .	....
OTHER COSTS	£ .	....
....	£ .	....
....	£ .	....

TOMORROW'S PLAN

....

....

....

....

....

CAMPER VAN
ROAD TRIP TRAVEL JOURNAL

DATE .... MILEAGE START ....

START TIME .... MILEAGE END ....

ARRIVAL TIME .... MILEAGE TOTAL ....

CAMPSITE NAME OR ....

WILDCAMPING LOCATION ....

ADDRESS 1 ....

ADDRESS 2 ....

GPS .... POST CODE ....

WHAT3WORDS ....

PHONE ....

E MAIL ....

WEBSITE WWW ....

MY RATING .... OUT OF 10   GOOD VALUE - YES / N0

WEATHER .... TEMPERATURE ....

NUMBER OF NIGHTS HERE .... RECOMMEND - YES / NO

DAILY COSTS	TODAY'S HIGHLIGHTS
SITE FEES £ .	....
FUEL £ .	....
LPG GAS £ .	....
GROCERIES £ .	....
EATING OUT £ .	....
ENTERTAINMENT £ .	....
OTHER COSTS £ .	....
.... £ .	....
.... £ .	....

TOMORROW'S PLAN

....

....

....

....

....

CAMPER VAN
ROAD TRIP TRAVEL JOURNAL

DATE .... MILEAGE START ....

START TIME .... MILEAGE END ....

ARRIVAL TIME .... MILEAGE TOTAL ....

CAMPSITE NAME OR ....

WILDCAMPING LOCATION ....

ADDRESS 1 ....

ADDRESS 2 ....

GPS .... POST CODE ....

WHAT3WORDS ....

PHONE ....

E MAIL ....

WEBSITE WWW ....

MY RATING .... OUT OF 10   GOOD VALUE - YES / N0

WEATHER .... TEMPERATURE ....

NUMBER OF NIGHTS HERE .... RECOMMEND - YES / NO

DAILY COSTS	TODAY'S HIGHLIGHTS
SITE FEES £ .	....
FUEL £ .	....
LPG GAS £ .	....
GROCERIES £ .	....
EATING OUT £ .	....
ENTERTAINMENT £ .	....
OTHER COSTS £ .	....
.... £ .	....
.... £ .	

TOMORROW'S PLAN

....

....

....

....

....

CAMPER VAN
ROAD TRIP TRAVEL JOURNAL

DATE .... MILEAGE START ....

START TIME .... MILEAGE END ....

ARRIVAL TIME .... MILEAGE TOTAL ....

CAMPSITE NAME OR ....

WILDCAMPING LOCATION ....

ADDRESS 1 ....

ADDRESS 2 ....

GPS .... POST CODE ....

WHAT3WORDS ....

PHONE ....

E MAIL ....

WEBSITE WWW ....

MY RATING .... OUT OF 10   GOOD VALUE - YES / N0

WEATHER .... TEMPERATURE ....

NUMBER OF NIGHTS HERE .... RECOMMEND - YES / NO

DAILY COSTS	TODAY'S HIGHLIGHTS
SITE FEES £ .	....
FUEL £ .	....
LPG GAS £ .	....
GROCERIES £ .	....
EATING OUT £ .	....
ENTERTAINMENT £ .	....
OTHER COSTS £ .	....
.... £ .	....
.... £ .	....

TOMORROW'S PLAN

....

....

....

....

....

CAMPER VAN
ROAD TRIP TRAVEL JOURNAL

DATE .... MILEAGE START ....

START TIME .... MILEAGE END ....

ARRIVAL TIME .... MILEAGE TOTAL ....

CAMPSITE NAME OR ....

WILDCAMPING LOCATION ....

ADDRESS 1 ....

ADDRESS 2 ....

GPS .... POST CODE ....

WHAT3WORDS ....

PHONE ....

E MAIL ....

WEBSITE WWW ....

MY RATING .... OUT OF 10   GOOD VALUE - YES / N0

WEATHER .... TEMPERATURE ....

NUMBER OF NIGHTS HERE .... RECOMMEND - YES / NO

DAILY COSTS		TODAY'S HIGHLIGHTS
SITE FEES	£ .	....
FUEL	£ .	....
LPG GAS	£ .	....
GROCERIES	£ .	....
EATING OUT	£ .	....
ENTERTAINMENT	£ .	....
OTHER COSTS	£ .	....
....	£ .	....
....	£ .	....

TOMORROW'S PLAN

....

....

....

....

....

CAMPER VAN
ROAD TRIP TRAVEL JOURNAL

DATE .... MILEAGE START ....
START TIME .... MILEAGE END ....
ARRIVAL TIME .... MILEAGE TOTAL ....

CAMPSITE NAME OR ....
WILDCAMPING LOCATION ....
ADDRESS 1 ....
ADDRESS 2 ....
GPS .... POST CODE ....
WHAT3WORDS ....
PHONE ....
E MAIL ....
WEBSITE WWW ....
MY RATING .... OUT OF 10   GOOD VALUE - YES / N0
WEATHER .... TEMPERATURE ....
NUMBER OF NIGHTS HERE .... RECOMMEND - YES / NO

DAILY COSTS		TODAY'S HIGHLIGHTS
SITE FEES	£ .	....
FUEL	£ .	....
LPG GAS	£ .	....
GROCERIES	£ .	....
EATING OUT	£ .	....
ENTERTAINMENT	£ .	....
OTHER COSTS	£ .	....
....	£ .	....
....	£ .	....

TOMORROW'S PLAN

....
....
....
....
....

CAMPER VAN
ROAD TRIP TRAVEL JOURNAL

DATE .... MILEAGE START ....

START TIME .... MILEAGE END ....

ARRIVAL TIME .... MILEAGE TOTAL ....

CAMPSITE NAME OR ....

WILDCAMPING LOCATION ....

ADDRESS 1 ....

ADDRESS 2 ....

GPS .... POST CODE ....

WHAT3WORDS ....

PHONE ....

E MAIL ....

WEBSITE WWW ....

MY RATING .... OUT OF 10   GOOD VALUE - YES / N0

WEATHER .... TEMPERATURE ....

NUMBER OF NIGHTS HERE .... RECOMMEND - YES / NO

DAILY COSTS		TODAY'S HIGHLIGHTS
SITE FEES	£ .	....
FUEL	£ .	....
LPG GAS	£ .	....
GROCERIES	£ .	....
EATING OUT	£ .	....
ENTERTAINMENT	£ .	....
OTHER COSTS	£ .	....
....	£ .	....
....	£ .	

TOMORROW'S PLAN

....

....

....

....

....

CAMPER VAN
ROAD TRIP TRAVEL JOURNAL

DATE .... MILEAGE START ....

START TIME .... MILEAGE END ....

ARRIVAL TIME .... MILEAGE TOTAL ....

CAMPSITE NAME OR ....

WILDCAMPING LOCATION ....

ADDRESS 1 ....

ADDRESS 2 ....

GPS .... POST CODE ....

WHAT3WORDS ....

PHONE ....

E MAIL ....

WEBSITE WWW ....

MY RATING .... OUT OF 10   GOOD VALUE - YES / N0

WEATHER .... TEMPERATURE ....

NUMBER OF NIGHTS HERE .... RECOMMEND - YES / NO

DAILY COSTS		TODAY'S HIGHLIGHTS
SITE FEES	£ .	....
FUEL	£ .	....
LPG GAS	£ .	....
GROCERIES	£ .	....
EATING OUT	£ .	....
ENTERTAINMENT	£ .	....
OTHER COSTS	£ .	....
....	£ .	....
....	£ .	....

TOMORROW'S PLAN

....

....

....

....

....

CAMPER VAN
ROAD TRIP TRAVEL JOURNAL

DATE .... MILEAGE START ....

START TIME .... MILEAGE END ....

ARRIVAL TIME .... MILEAGE TOTAL ....

CAMPSITE NAME OR ....

WILDCAMPING LOCATION ....

ADDRESS 1 ....

ADDRESS 2 ....

GPS .... POST CODE ....

WHAT3WORDS ....

PHONE ....

E MAIL ....

WEBSITE WWW ....

MY RATING .... OUT OF 10   GOOD VALUE - YES / N0

WEATHER .... TEMPERATURE ....

NUMBER OF NIGHTS HERE .... RECOMMEND - YES / NO

DAILY COSTS	TODAY'S HIGHLIGHTS
SITE FEES £ .	....
FUEL £ .	....
LPG GAS £ .	....
GROCERIES £ .	....
EATING OUT £ .	....
ENTERTAINMENT £ .	....
OTHER COSTS £ .	....
.... £ .	....
.... £ .	....

TOMORROW'S PLAN

....

....

....

....

....

CAMPER VAN
ROAD TRIP TRAVEL JOURNAL

DATE .... MILEAGE START ....

START TIME .... MILEAGE END ....

ARRIVAL TIME .... MILEAGE TOTAL ....

CAMPSITE NAME OR ....

WILDCAMPING LOCATION ....

ADDRESS 1 ....

ADDRESS 2 ....

GPS .... POST CODE ....

WHAT3WORDS ....

PHONE ....

E MAIL ....

WEBSITE WWW ....

MY RATING .... OUT OF 10   GOOD VALUE - YES / N0

WEATHER .... TEMPERATURE ....

NUMBER OF NIGHTS HERE .... RECOMMEND - YES / NO

DAILY COSTS		TODAY'S HIGHLIGHTS
SITE FEES	£ .	....
FUEL	£ .	....
LPG GAS	£ .	....
GROCERIES	£ .	....
EATING OUT	£ .	....
ENTERTAINMENT	£ .	....
OTHER COSTS	£ .	....
.... £ .		....
.... £ .		....

TOMORROW'S PLAN

....

....

....

....

....

CAMPER VAN
ROAD TRIP TRAVEL JOURNAL

DATE ....   MILEAGE START ....

START TIME ....   MILEAGE END ....

ARRIVAL TIME ....   MILEAGE TOTAL ....

CAMPSITE NAME OR ....

WILDCAMPING LOCATION ....

ADDRESS 1 ....

ADDRESS 2 ....

GPS .... POST CODE ....

WHAT3WORDS ....

PHONE ....

E MAIL ....

WEBSITE WWW ....

MY RATING .... OUT OF 10   GOOD VALUE - YES / N0

WEATHER .... TEMPERATURE ....

NUMBER OF NIGHTS HERE .... RECOMMEND - YES / NO

DAILY COSTS		TODAY'S HIGHLIGHTS
SITE FEES	£ .	....
FUEL	£ .	....
LPG GAS	£ .	....
GROCERIES	£ .	....
EATING OUT	£ .	....
ENTERTAINMENT	£ .	....
OTHER COSTS	£ .	....
....	£ .	....
....	£ .	....

TOMORROW'S PLAN

....

....

....

....

....

CAMPER VAN
ROAD TRIP TRAVEL JOURNAL

DATE .... MILEAGE START ....

START TIME .... MILEAGE END ....

ARRIVAL TIME .... MILEAGE TOTAL ....

CAMPSITE NAME OR ....

WILDCAMPING LOCATION ....

ADDRESS 1 ....

ADDRESS 2 ....

GPS .... POST CODE ....

WHAT3WORDS ....

PHONE ....

E MAIL ....

WEBSITE WWW ....

MY RATING .... OUT OF 10   GOOD VALUE - YES / N0

WEATHER .... TEMPERATURE ....

NUMBER OF NIGHTS HERE .... RECOMMEND - YES / NO

DAILY COSTS	TODAY'S HIGHLIGHTS
SITE FEES £ .	....
FUEL £ .	....
LPG GAS £ .	....
GROCERIES £ .	....
EATING OUT £ .	....
ENTERTAINMENT £ .	....
OTHER COSTS £ .	....
.... £ .	....
.... £ .	....

TOMORROW'S PLAN

....

....

....

....

....

Printed in Great Britain
by Amazon

13241377R00058